ENGLISH PANORAMA

By the same author

TOWN AND COUNTRYSIDE
TOWN PLANNING
THE ANATOMY OF THE VILLAGE
OXFORD REPLANNED
CATHEDRAL CITY
EXETER PHOENIX
NEWER SARUM
GEORGIAN CITY
A DERELICT AREA

and others

Given to the Department of Architecture, University of Nebraska in respect of the program "Observation Nebraska" in the Civic Design Course, in the hope of stimulating an appreciation of the richness of your inheritance —— and the dangers that beset it

Patrick Horsbrugh.
January 196

ENGLISH
PANORAMA

THOMAS SHARP

THE ARCHITECTURAL PRESS
London

To
M. K. W.

First published by J. M. Dent & Sons Ltd., 1936
This edition, revised, newly illustrated and entirely reset,
published by The Architectural Press, 1950

CONTENTS

ILLUSTRATIONS

ENGRAVINGS AND DRAWINGS IN THE TEXT

ACKNOWLEDGEMENTS

The author expresses his thanks to the following who have supplied photographs and engravings for the illustrations: Aerofilms Ltd., pp. 127, 138; The Architectural Press, pp. 11 (top), 126, 128, 133, 135 (top), 141-3, 145-6, 147 (top), 148; Mr. Erich Auerbach, p. 139; Bournville Village Trust, p. 140; Central Office of Information, p. 9; *Country Life*, pp. 10, 125 (top); Mr. Alfred Cracknell, p. 148; Messrs. Dell & Wainwright, pp. 12, 126, 128, 135, 142, 143, 144, 146, 147; Miss Daisy Edis, p. 123; Mr. Herbert Felton, pp. 122, 134 (top), 145; Mr. A. G. Sheppard Fidler, p. 141 (bottom); Messrs. F. Frith & Co. Ltd., p. 125 (bottom); Mr. Frederick Gibberd, pp. 5, 144; Messrs. Hobbs & Sons, p. 132 (bottom); The Housing Centre, p. 141 (top); Lever Brothers & Unilever Limited, p. 85; National Buildings Record, pp. 130 (bottom), 131; Picture Post Library, pp. 35, 40, 59; Royal Institute of British Architects, pp. 72, 73; Studio Lisa p. 147 (bottom); Mr. Will F. Taylor, pp. 130 (top), 134; *The Times*, pp. 11 (bottom), 135 (bottom); Town Planning Institute, pp. 12, 31, 45, 67; Messrs. Worthington, p. 124.

1. Town and Countryside: Gloucester and Gloucestershire

2. (*Above*) *Cathedral City: Chichester*

3. (*Opposite top*) *Monumental City: Bath*
4. (*Opposite bottom*) *Industrial City: Staffordshire Potteries*

5. (*Above*) *New Town, Harlow*

CHAPTER ONE

INTRODUCTORY

OF ALL THE PECULIARITIES of the English scene none is more striking than the contrast between the quality of its urban and its rural parts. The countryside is generally acknowledged to have a very special beauty. Even in its geological form and climate England seems a particularly favoured plot of earth. Its gentle undulations offer an infinite variety of prospect. It is blessed with a thousand rivers and streams. Mild suns and soft rains continually refresh its verdure. Nature was in a beneficent mood when it created this island where, as William Morris wrote, " all is measured, mingled, varied, gliding easily one thing into another".

But the charm of the English rural scene lies in more than these characteristics. It lies in the intimacy, in the sense of order and design which everywhere pervade it. The landscape has, indeed, a *composed* quality. Trees and hedges give it a rhythmic pattern. Village and hamlet, cottage and hall, set securely within it seem to display a deep accord between man and Nature. There is about it the quietness and certainty of age and custom. It has a lived-in character; the appearance of a thing used lovingly, with understanding and pride. It is a humanised landscape. It is the landscape of a high civilization.

The contrast of this countryside with many of the towns that are scattered about it is startling. For the most part the older towns show much of the quality of grace and something of the sense of order which the countryside displays. But the towns of the last hundred and fifty years—and they constitute at least nine-tenths of the urban scenes of England—do not. It might be expected that above all it would be the town, which as distinct from the countryside is man's own personal deliberate creation *from nothing*, that should display high qualities of order and design, that should be humanised, that should reflect his pride and civilization. It is not so now in England. Most of our towns are mean, squalid, squandering: they have neither form nor order, let alone beauty. In comparison with the civilized country-side they seem to represent the landscape of barbarism.

This contrast is so obvious and yet so curious that generations of Englishmen, to say nothing of multitudes of bewildered foreigners, have found it necessary to invent some explanation for it; some explanation, of course, that was not too derogatory, that did not empha-size too deeply the fact that while Englishmen of the last 150 years have been unfortunate in their urban creations many other people have managed a good deal better. But even an Englishman may without shame confess to being a little lower than the angels, especially when one of his poets has provided a tag which resolves the difficulty as neatly as does the gentle Cowper's famous line. So the fact that "God made the country and man made the town" has for long seemed at the same time a sufficient excuse for the unpleasantness of our towns and a modest disclaimer of any responsibility for the beauty of our countryside.

Unfortunately, this explanation will not bear more than a moment's examination. God made the country! Maybe: but not the English country. The country that God made was primeval forest, swamp, jungle, prairie and desolate moor. His landscape was gigantic, wild and terrible. There is little of it left in any civilized part of the world to-day: there is hardly a square mile of it remaining in England.

But if this explanation will not do, and if we are thus

14

deprived of the satisfaction of giving God the praise and ourselves the blame, what then? Well, if God Himself may not be directly accredited with the English countryside, there are yet other fine-sounding phrases that may be offered to explain this troublesome contrast between it and our towns. There is, for example, that explanation advanced by a polite German professor who in a broadcast lecture some years ago spoke of the 'time-made England' he saw in the countryside, and of the 'man-made England' he saw in the restless, grimy, utilitarian manufacturing districts. This explanation at least has its point, for it hints at any rate at a half-truth; and if the professor had said 'time-matured' instead of 'time-made' he might eventually have stumbled upon a more accurate definition, though since he did not do this his classification can only be regarded at best as an evasion.

And now, being deprived of both God and Time as shelters for his modesty, and wearied in any case by an enquiry which seems to lead nowhere, the ordinary Englishman would probably shrug his shoulders and be finally content to explain the contrast of his urban and rural scenes by saying that we have never really been a nation of town-dwellers, but are countrymen at heart and have centred all our affections on the countryside. Which, however false it may be as an argument, gives at least some hint of the truth that the English country-side was made, not by God, nor by Time, nor by mere Accident, but by the Englishman himself—who was also the maker of towns.

It is obvious, indeed, that all civilized landscapes are largely man-made, or at any rate man-directed. Everywhere man alters and adapts to suit his own requirements the scenes within which his life is set. He would never have emerged from barbarism had he not done so. When once he left off his nomadic wanderings to settle permanently in some chosen place he immediately began to interfere on quite an extensive scale with that "wilderness grotesque and wild" which was the country that God made. He was bound to; his physical survival depended upon it. And as the social structure of his society developed he began more and more, and in an increasing variety of ways, to change the pattern of the earth's surface, to modify the wild natural scene. Thus the prime motive of man's activities in the landscape has always been, and is to-day, an economic one.

In most parts of the world it is even now the sole motive. But there is another activity by which another and a higher facet of man's progress towards civilization may be expressed. In this activity, he deliberately adapts, out of spiritual desire, the bald pattern which his economic activity has created: he exercises conscious design towards the creation of a landscape that will satisfy his æsthetic as well as his economic needs, that will be a home as well as a workplace.

This conscious æsthetic design, however, is a quality which few people have found indispensable to their existence or worth the material sacrifice which it entails. Consequently it is unusual on anything but the smallest scale. In most countries where it has been exercised it has been limited to the isolated estates where great personages have sought to make special places for their own delight and glory. Only in one country has it been applied in any large-scale form to the everyday landscape. It has been so applied in England. And so the English countryside is probably the most highly humanised landscape in the world.

And because it is the most humanised by its own people, it is also the most individualised of landscapes. And it is upon its humanised quality that its charm, both for its own inhabitants and for foreigners, almost entirely depends. No other landscape has the friendliness of the English landscape, none its satisfying sense of security. Most are little more than the outward settings of human life, the theatres of man's age-old struggle for existence, the incidental scenes of economic activity. Even where they have been lived in for thousands of years they are still terrifying though tamed, still unfriendly though familiarised. They have not yet been brought into a satisfying human relationship. Man lives and works there as an infinitesimally small creature in a vast unbounded space, the mere man with a hoe, the humble worm of hymnology. The scale of most landscapes is still gigantic and oppressive, is still cruelly destructive of man's stature.

The landscape of England is very different from these. Here, except on a few mountain ranges or on stretches of moorland and heath, which serve but as a foil for the more normal scenes—here there are no vast distances to overwhelm man with his littleness. Here space has been conquered, the terrifying scale of Nature has been reduced. And this miracle has been accomplished by the simplest of means. Never was there so modest a formula for a work so productive of human happiness. On a wide unbroken expanse the great surrounding distances oppress one with their monotony and with a feeling of one's own insignificance. If the vast arena be broken up and subdivided by ditches, as it is in many landscapes, there is little difference. If it be subdivided by open fencing it becomes only a little less terrible. But divided into small fields, hedged with natural solid visible boundaries, the gigantic world becomes a comfortable and friendly place. Distance is brought within easy comprehension, vastness is reduced to a succession of small units, the apparently infinite is rounded to a pattern and a rhythm that is an echo of the pattern of human life itself.

And when the instrument of this stupendous work has in itself the beauty that the familiar hawthorn hedges of England have, and when to the assistance of this instrument is brought another, used as effectively as are the hedgerow trees and the little copses and woodlands of our happy land, it is small wonder that this landscape which we have inherited should be regarded by many people as one of the supreme achievements of civilization.

But if the English countryside is indeed man-made, that merely makes the contrast between it and the majority of our towns the more surprising. How comes it that the nation which in this one matter could display such imagination, such a passion for beauty, could be so blind and so barbarous as to create that other part of the English scene, those dreary and dreadful towns that are as much a disgrace to our civilization as the countryside is a credit? The truth of the matter is, of course, that though it was the same nation which created these things it was not the same generations of men. It could not be, for if the will to beauty exists, or even the lowlier sense of design which results in mere orderliness, that will does not express itself only in dealing with one specially loved object, but is so deep a part of the very being of the creator that it is manifest in his other activities, and controls his attitude to teapots no less than his attitude to towns, and to towns as well as to trees.

And so, in point of fact, those few generations of eighteenth- and early-nineteenth-century Englishmen who created beauty in the countryside created also beauty of a no less striking order in their towns. The quality of their works in the two parts of the scene showed no contrast: it was of the same high excellence: it was prompted by the same imagination, the same instinctive will towards beauty and order, the same understanding of the inherent possibilities of each medium for the expression of the civilization of its creators.

The contrast which we see between the qualities of the urban and rural landscapes to-day arises out of the superimposing of the works of succeeding generations upon these earlier achievements, and upon the unequal incidence of these accretions on the separate parts. If the activities of these later generations had been more equally distributed over the towns and the countryside, there is no doubt that there would be little of that contrast in quality which is now so obvious: instead of there being a beautiful countryside and some hundreds of dreary and ugly towns, the whole scene would have been one of equal dreariness.

Fortunately, the activities of the generations that created the foul towns were by various factors limited to the urban part of the scene. Under those activities much of the beauty of most of the older towns was altogether overwhelmed, so that the fact that the English had once known the art of urban design passed almost completely out of mind. But the countryside, at least, survived this particular lapse into barbarism. Survived it, alas, only to fall before another—the recent one. For the lack of knowledge (e.g. of a flexible form of mechanical transport) which limited nineteenth-century industrial developments to the towns has now been filled by the discovery of the internal combustion engine. So we, being in this matter only a little less barbarous than the Victorians, were until lately undertaking in the countryside destruction which they could not bring about. And soon, no doubt, unless we redeem ourselves, we shall no longer have the embarrassment of accounting for the contrasting qualities of the two parts of the English scene, for there will be no contrast to account for, but only a universal meanness.

§

The purpose of this essay is to tell briefly the story of the evolution of the English landscape from its primeval state to its present complex humanisation, and to indicate the motives that have prompted man's activity at the various well-marked stages of that evolution. The story itself is of some interest; for, since in his physical environment is expressed man's cultural as well as his social and political state, a landscape is an index to a civilization. But chiefly, at this time of change and uncertainty, the value of the story lies in the way it may point out for our future guidance those lines of activity which in the past have led to fine achievement and those which have led to disaster. Now, with the acquisition of extensive new powers of town and country planning, is the time to change the lines along which our recent activity was so wrongly directed; and a study of the countryside which we have been destroying, and the towns which we unfortunately have not, may do much to make us realise the extent of our stupidity in the past thirty years or so.

CHAPTER TWO

THE EARLY AND MEDIÆVAL SCENE

AT SOME DARK UNKNOWN PERIOD after the passing
of the Ice Age, primitive man established himself, and
developed through the stages of hunter and shepherd, on
the grass-covered highlands above the area of swamp
and forest that was taking the final form and con-
figuration of the present British Isles. Infinitely slowly
through the static centuries he developed in these places,
shaking off the beast from which he had arisen; rising,
falling, rising again to acquire some new defence against
the awful enmity of the natural world that surrounded
him. Over an unimaginably long period of time his dull
brain gradually found ways of using natural things
against Nature herself, discovering fire, discovering
metal and shaping it into the tools that won him his
slow supremacy. So eventually he emerged from the
solitary figure wandering darkly and fearfully in all the
bewildering chaos of the early world to the settled
tribesman who at last was beginning to till the earth
and enrich his life with its rewards.

Through all the long dawn of history early man played
his small part in the subjugation of the primeval wilderness, each new race extending and losing, but always in
the long run extending a little further, the rights that
their forerunners had won over the natural world;
until eventually the Briton and his immediate pre-
decessors not only continued to clear here and there a
patch of forest as men had done for thousands of years
before them, but began to undertake creative works,
some of which have left their mark even on the landscape

D

of to-day. Thus they founded settlements over whose sites men are still occupied in going about their business of living; they developed primitive trackways which still survive, raised crude monuments and formed cultivation terraces of which vestiges still remain to incite curious men to vain speculation. Yet, after all this, the results of these thousands of years of activity, judged as landscape development and measured in terms of the whole country, were so small in their scale and so primitive in their scope that, in so far as their effect on the evolution of the natural scene is concerned, they can hardly be said to have existed at all.

It was not until the Roman came that any conscious attempt was made to impose some order and system upon the wilderness of England. He, the possessor in his native countryside of a landscape that had been humanised for centuries, set about bringing something of the convenience and comforts of home into this barbarous land. He built his magnificent roads that still drive up hill and down dale, carrying to-day a traffic undreamed of by their creators. He built his forts and camps, and that great wall that still strides the Northumbrian moorlands. But most of all, he colonised the countryside with his villas and brought to the cultivation of the land a settled and scientific agricultural system that changed completely the appearance of many of the old forest clearings. And one thing especially did he do that has a deep interest for us to-day, for it was he who first employed for the enclosure of land those hawthorn hedges which are now the commonest features of the countryside (though he employed them to a limited extent only, about the gardens of his villas).

It has been claimed for the Roman that it was he also who first brought to England the idea of towns. But if a town may be properly defined as "a locality the population of which, instead of working the soil, devotes itself to commercial activity", then towns probably did not exist in England, or indeed in any part of northern Europe, before mediæval times.* The Roman 'towns' whose plans can still be traced in the streets of a few of our older cities were hardly towns at all in this commercial sense. There were mostly fortresses, permanent camps, administrative centres. When they lapsed from those uses, they lay deserted for centuries, crumbling gradually into decay, most of them never again to be inhabited but doomed to disappear and leave scarcely a trace behind them.

The Roman's contribution to the English scene was therefore largely a rural one. But even under him the cultivated area of the country was a very small fraction of the whole; and much even of that must have lapsed again to forest and jungle during the dark centuries which followed his withdrawal. It was the Saxon who exerted by far the most powerful influence on all this early landscape development. Certainly it was his social system of hamlet and manor, with its common field method of agriculture, that determined the appearance of the countryside and kept it more or less fixed for a thousand years, except in so far as it was changed by the clearance of the forest and the taming of the waste.

Yet early Saxon England was still only slightly removed from the wild. Vast forests covered most of the land, occasionally varied by brown marshes and bogs encircling great shallow fens, or by a few bare uplands standing above the tangled wilderness. Here and there the monotony of the landscape was broken by a clearing where crouched a mud and wattle hamlet. Next to the hamlet, or sometimes a slight distance away by the banks of a stream, were the common meadows; and right round stretched the hedgeless expanse of the common arable fields that were cropped year after year in an unvarying succession of compulsory rotations. Beyond this ranged the common pasture: and then,

*Pirenne: *Mediæval Cities*.

encircling all, the forest; thinned at first where herds of swine rummaged for mast, then thick black and impenetrable. No separate farms and few villages broke upon the scene: there were only the small hamlets that were completely isolated and shut away, where small communities worked in common and lived and died with so little movement that even the great Roman roads were absorbed again into the forest.

More steadily now, the clearance of the forest progressed, until, by the time of the Norman conquest, parts of the south at least had reached a fair stage of development. Indeed, if Domesday Book is to be believed, there were counties in the south where, in the eleventh century, the amount of arable land was actually in excess of what it was in the 1930's. And certainly by this time the villages in the more settled parts were no longer so isolated: sometimes they were so close together that a pasture ground was common to two or more. But, even so, vast areas of the country and practically all parts of the north were in their primeval state.

The Saxon had raised a few stone-built churches. One or two, humble and earthy, remain to us still. Nothing remains of his houses. He built temporarily: he was still close to the earth, still subdued to Nature. But now the Norman inaugurated a new attitude towards the natural scene. Partly out of necessity and partly out of his defiant character, he entered into competition with the natural landscape. Castle and cathedral rose on the hill-top, above the forest, subduing it. The Saxon had modified the scene by altering natural conditions: the Norman began a new process of dominating it with artificial forms.

It was through the Norman also that England acquired its first genuine towns. Under his rule the pulse of the national life quickened, men acquired new social habits, and trade began to develop on a far wider scale than had existed hitherto, if indeed it can be said to have existed

24

at all. These early towns were in reality but suburbs of fortresses. They were composed chiefly of the houses of merchants and others who attached themselves to the patronage of some nobleman and settled under the protection of his stronghold. But though ultimately dependent for their existence upon the shelter of castle walls, these 'towns' themselves were generally enclosed against surprise attack, their defence works consisting of stout wooden palisades very like those of the forts and blockhouses built by European emigrants in America in the seventeenth and eighteenth centuries. Their very form is now a matter for conjecture. Probably all that can be said of them is that there would be a market near the banks of the stream that ran by, and that the principal streets all ran between this market and the town gates, and so to the open country beyond. The sole relic of these towns that still survives is in the heraldic custom of symbolising a city with a kind of circular hedge. Here in these squalid tangles of crowded hovels, urban civilization was already slowly advancing, though as yet there was little outward expression of its essentially co-operative basis.

Nor was there much more in the far larger and more numerous towns which developed from the twelfth century onwards. These had a sturdier and more independent life. They were no longer founded on some warlord's patronage. Their foundation was, in the long run, much more secure. It was in wool. Soon wool and its manufacture into cloths and worsteds became the premier industry in England; and it is probably true to say that right down till towards the end of the eighteenth century most towns and the majority of villages owed their existence mainly to this commodity.

This development of manufacture amounted to an early industrial revolution, and it was accompanied by a mixture of cause and effect not unlike that which created so great an upheaval five or six centuries later.

And while it exerted a determining influence on the development of the early towns, it had an even greater effect on the appearance of the countryside.

The Norman, though he had inaugurated a new building tradition and had founded our first towns, had perpetuated the old agricultural system, altering it only to the extent that where, before, the hamlet had been a co-operative community, it now became a bonded slavish instrument for the profit of the manor. So for centuries the clearing of the forest went slowly forward and the open field system continued; and, except for the slow reduction of the waste lands, the appearance of the country remained the same. Everywhere in the cultivated areas there was a remarkable preponderance of arable, and hardly anywhere were there any permanent enclosures, save for a few round the gardens and orchards of the villages, or round the paddocks where the young stock was kept.

The first slight departures from this system began towards the end of the thirteenth century. In 1235 the Statute of Merton asserted the lord of the manor's proprietary interest in the common waste, and some fifty years later another statute, that of Westminster the Second, gave him power to inclose the common lands against his tenants. These powers were to be invoked long afterwards to strengthen claims for inclosure (that is, for the drawing into separate ownerships of land hitherto held or used in common); but they can have been little used at this time, for it is certain that the change in the agricultural system which their use would have entailed did not occur to any extent for several centuries. Probably the most they did at the time was to furnish the lord with a deer park and perhaps occasionally with an inclosed farm which operated side by side with the common fields.

The first real departure from the old agricultural economy (and therefore the first considerable change in

Common fields in the 13th century.

the appearance of humanised countryside) came with the Black Death, a century later. When that scourge had carried off half the population of the country, it was natural that it should affect the supply of labour. But while it reduced the number of their labourers, it increased the size of the landowners' estates, since, when whole families died, their common rights passed over to the lord of the manor. Following these changing influences there were others. These arose out of the growing trade in wool. Already in the fifteenth century, industry, with the freedom and pleasures it offered in the towns, was proving more attractive than husbandry to the more adventurous members of the oppressed labouring classes. This in itself assisted in the natural expansion of the industry and in an increased demand for its raw materials, while this increased demand in turn produced an agrarian revolution in which the substitution of wool-raising for corn-growing led to inclosures that not only had their effect in a change of landscape but drove further large numbers of agricultural labourers into the towns. Thus under these influences something still far removed from but yet akin

27

to the present English countryside began slowly and faintly to emerge in some parts of the country.

Despite these changes, however, a great part of the country was still in an unredeemed primeval state. In the fifteenth century an unbroken series of woods and fens stretched northwards across England between Lincoln and the Mersey. The great eastern fens covered hundred of thousands of acres: north and south of them extended vast areas of bog and swamp. Yorkshire was swamp, heath, forest and bare moorland. Lancashire was largely marsh and peat moss. Warwickshire, Northamptonshire and Leicestershire were covered with forest. Sherwood Forest covered nearly the whole of Nottinghamshire; much of Sussex was still the forest of Andredsweald; Cannock Chase was crowded with oaks; the Chiltern district of Buckingham and Oxford was thick with woods—and so on over most of the country.* In some counties there were now great clearings; but where the landscape was not waste and wild, it was generally quite open: it was also scrubby and patchy in effect, and seen from the air it would probably have had the appearance of a vast area of modern allotment gardens (though without their squalid sheds).

Slowly the initial breaking down of the open-field system continued throughout the Tudor period. In the reigns of Henry VIII and Edward VI, especially, commons and open fields disappeared in many places, and the country saw the first notable instalment of inclosure. Under the continually increasing demand for wool it also saw a steady conversion of arable land to pasture. The writings of the times are full of complaints of injustice resulting from the one and hardship from the other. "Where there have been many householders and inhabitants there is now but a shepherd and his dog," said Bishop Latimer. And later, in 1540, "such store is set on cattle in every place", wrote Harrison, "that the

*Curtler: *History of Agriculture.*

28

fourth part of the land is scarcely manured for grain." Even the statutes and the royal commissions of the times reflect the changing conditions of the countryside. Laws were passed limiting the possessions of one person in sheep, against the conversion of arable land into pasture, against the pulling down of farmhouses: all of which, and many others, must have been generally evaded, for in spite of pious official and unofficial expressions of concern, the very instruments which made the changes possible, the Statutes of Merton and Westminster the Second, were confirmed and re-enacted.

All these changes in the countryside brought increasing prosperity and power to the towns. At first this industrial revolution (when once it was firmly established after many vicissitudes) naturally resulted in a rapid expansion of the existing centres of population—rapid, that is, in comparison to their slow growth, almost their stagnation, through previous centuries (for it is very necessary to remember how small were even the most important of these mediæval cities: Lincoln, for example, though among the first half-dozen cities in the kingdom, had a population of less than 3,500 towards the end of the fourteenth century; Leicester had only some 2,000; Oxford had under 2,500: so that all of them were but little larger than the smallest country towns of to-day). But probably the greatest effect of this new industrialisation was in the establishment of numbers of new towns and villages either on virgin sites or around older hamlet settlements. The jealousy of the existing town guilds could not in the long run keep out of the trade the great numbers of workers who now, through choice or necessity, flocked into the towns. It merely resulted in consolidating competition in new places. So Leland about 1540 could describe parts of the country as being covered with a network of 'clothing towns' and 'clothing villages'. Here in this long-continued and widespread manufacture of cloth lies the reason not only for that

29

great number of small towns which is so notable and pleasant a feature of England, but for the lack of a sharp distinction between town and village which is also so characteristic of the English scene.

From contemporary records we can still catch vivid glimpses of the busy and eager life which was lived in these towns. And in the still-existing cathedral cities, especially, we can to-day see actual examples of the buildings where the wealth and pride of the chief citizens were displayed, in the churches, the richly-wrought guildhalls, and the larger houses of the merchant princes. Nevertheless it is difficult to form any clear picture of what those towns looked like as a whole. Though their street patterns have survived with remarkable purity in many places, the street frontages have been over-laid with the buildings of succeeding generations. For the most part the town streets of even the later part of the mediæval period must have been almost entirely unorganised jumbles of strongly individualised buildings of wildly differing heights and sizes, individual buildings that were innocent of any expression of communal feeling, that generally showed no more recognition of the street than that it was a necessary passageway for communication. And certainly those passageways were very different from the paved spaces of, say, York's Shambles as we see them to-day. Then they functioned as open sewers and garbage dumps as well as thoroughfares. They were unpaved, uncleansed and unlighted. And they were by no means as continuously built-up as they later became. The crowded condition of the mediæval town has probably been much exaggerated: certainly in England, where the necessity for protection lapsed much earlier than it did elsewhere, most towns tended to grow out beyond the defences, leaving large unbuilt-on spaces of orchards and gardens and even farmyards within the city walls.

Yet even when due allowance is made for the contri-

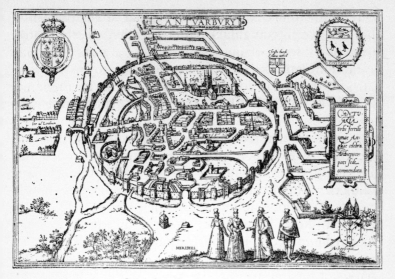

Canterbury in the 17th century.

bution of later buildings to the 'mediæval' street scenes that remain to-day, and acknowledging too that there was much that was squalid and mean in the later as well as in the earlier mediæval town, there can be no doubt that the best of these towns were wonderfully rich and lively in their physical form. They were full of the most subtle as well as the most exciting pictorial effects. These effects are so striking and so similarly achieved in scores of towns in different parts of Europe that some later observers* have maintained that they must have been deliberately planned. That is highly unlikely. While sites for important buildings were no doubt chosen with care, and while the full pictorial possibilities of those sites must often have been consciously and deliberately exploited to the utmost, the form that was given to the *new* towns which are known to have been planned at this time is in itself proof to the contrary. These new towns

*e.g. Camillo Sitte in *Der Stadtebau*, 1889.

31

were deliberately planned to a regular street pattern—
that simple rectangular pattern which is the most
elementary form of land subdivision, a form that has
been commonly used in laying-out new towns in most
parts of the world for thousands of years. In England,
as early as the beginning of the twelfth century, the new
town of Ludlow, built under the shadow of a fortress,
displayed in the rectangular system of its streets the
existence of a preconceived plan which controlled the
lines of its development. And so did others which
followed. The Plantagenets, especially, became active
in the conscious founding of new cities. Henry II
founded New Woodstock; John founded Liverpool;
Richard founded Portsmouth. And most of all Edward I,
towards the end of the thirteenth century, displayed the
genius of his line in this direction. At Flint, Rhuddlan,
Carnarvon, Beaumaris and Conway he founded and
developed garrison towns to keep the turbulent Welsh
subdued. These places may not perhaps be classified as
normal towns, but rather in the same category of military
and administrative centres as were the Roman camps;
but in the founding of Kingstown-on-Hull in 1293 (for
the building of which the art of brick-making, which
had been dead since the Roman occupation, is said to
have been revived), and in the rebuilding of Winchelsea
on a new site when the old town had been washed away
by the sea, Edward showed himself to be the first
genuine town-planner whom England had yet produced.
And besides this royal activity there were other under-
takings, such as the transplanting of Salisbury from its
windswept and waterless hilltop to begin life anew among
the meadows of a kindlier situation, which make the
thirteenth century memorable in the annals of pre-
Renaissance town planning. But every single example
in all this succession of new towns was laid out on the
common-place grid-iron pattern: and it is impossible to
believe that the people who consciously planned these

32

places could consciously plan the very different broad effects that are characteristic of the more typical mediæval urban scene, even though it is likely that individual effects arising from the siting of individual buildings were carefully considered and deliberately created.

These scenes had a dramatic effectiveness and a pictorial liveliness which was entirely lacking in a planned town such as Salisbury, for when streets are twisting and tortuous they hold far more secrets and sustain the interest far longer than when they are straight. In the straight street all is obvious, immediately apprehensible. But the winding street is full of changing incident, is charged with surprise, is tense with the possibilities of drama. Round the next bend the narrow shadowed street may suddenly debouch into an open square full of sunshine. In the square itself there is the sense of at least a local climax, for the tortuous streets leading out of it curve away so quickly that their openings hardly disturb the continuity of the street frontages, the sense of enclosure. Or it may actually be that one suddenly comes upon a major, not merely a minor, climax—the cathedral in its close, the guildhall in the market place. Everywhere in the mediæval town there was variety for the accustomed eye, and continuous interest and surprise for the stranger. And it all came naturally, incidentally—which was what gave particular point to it. The pictorial drama of the mediæval town was not organised: it unfolded itself. There was no conscious preparation for effect: no deliberate architectural build-up. The splendours were almost casual. And therein, indeed, lay much of the richness. When the small elbowed the big, the almshouses alongside the cathedral, the little shops on either side of the guildhall, the cottages adjoining the college, they did not prejudice its effect, they enhanced it; they magnified its scale: by way of contrast between the lowly and the noble,

33

between the humble and the rich, they increased nobility and richness in the buildings to which they acted as foils.

Of all the squalor and the casual splendour of the mediæval town, only occasional and much changed glimpses of the splendour remain—and even in these it is often merely the plan-form, and the effects of drama and movement that it produces, which reflect the spirit of the mediæval town, as it is reflected in some hundreds of market places up and down the country where hardly a single mediæval building survives. An occasional approximation to the real scene can be caught in such a street as Mercery Lane at Canterbury, where the narrow curving over-hung street opens out into a little square before the richly-wrought gateway to the close of the cathedral, whose pinnacled towers, though rising beyond the main street picture, have nevertheless dominated it all the way down. Here in a small space is contained the quintessence of all the pictorial subtleties that characterized the mediæval street—variety, incident, surprise, intimacy, intricacy, enclosure, drama, contrast, subsidiary climax, delayed climax, and more. Some of these qualities, and especially the drama, the sense of delayed climax and the thrill of surprise, are seen in an almost breath-taking way at Durham, that dirty dilapidated city whose inherent nobility is such that not even a hundred years of brutal neglect has seriously impaired it. There the approach to the cathedral is up a long narrow steeply-climbing street in which no glimpse of the great building is seen, until another street, even steeper, narrower, more winding, opens up, with a view of the western towers beyond, in middle distance. Then, at the top of the short hill, at the head of the curve, the confined view having thus far excited one's expectations, the street suddenly opens out into a great level square, broad, spacious, elevated, with a wide expanse of sky: and there, dramatically, in

34

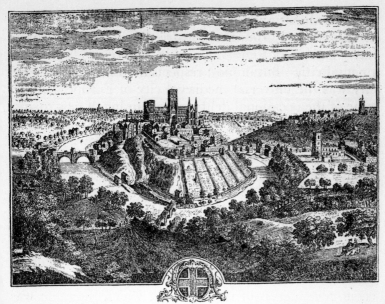

Durham : from an 18th-century engraving.

one moment, the whole fine length of the great cathedral, framed by low buildings along the two sides of the square, is displayed to the astonished view.

These, and some others like them which still remain, were special, not the ordinary, scenes. In the more ordinary mediæval town the pictorial effects, the drama, the liveliness, the sense of movement and the other attributes, were inevitably on a less exciting plane: and everywhere the squalor was far more frequent than the splendour. But nevertheless these were the attributes that were in some degree or other common to all: and it is these that mark mediæval town-building off from the town-building of other periods, in England as elsewhere.

None of these characteristics of the mediæval town was peculiarly English, though one or two particular forms, such as the sequestration of the cathedral in its own close away from the secular streets, were highly individualised; and, in addition, such special conditions as the freedom from the constriction of city walls must have produced some noticeable difference from continental cities. But in most respects the English mediæval city was the universal mediæval city of Europe. And in spite of the occasional deliberate planning of new towns, and in spite of all the striking pictorial characteristics that have been described, the mediæval town was not the creation of a people who had realised more than dimly the possibilities of organising the environment of their lives. If men associated in towns and profited by their association, it was still largely the involuntary association of the herd rather than of an ordered society.

The countryside displayed the same characteristics. Everywhere men were still too close to the early struggle for existence to be concerned with more than the economic interest of the scenes in which their life was set. They had not yet learned to look upon the visible world with the eyes of creators. They were opportunists rather, snatching here and there what comfort or happiness they could in a world full of fear and insecurity. Doubts and superstitions still hid from them the glory of their domination of the material world. That world was still fearful to their half-opened eyes.

But the slow awakening of the Renaissance was already at hand.

CHAPTER THREE

THE RENAISSANCE: THE HUMANISED SCENE

THE IMPORTANCE OF THE RENAISSANCE lies less in the direct knowledge that it brought than in the mental attitude which it engendered. This is particularly so in connection with the landscape of both town and country. It brought little new knowledge to aid man in the tilling of his fields or in the work that necessitated his living together in towns; but it brought a new outlook that very gradually, but nevertheless completely, changed the appearance of the places in which those activities were conducted. In that long slow awakening men arrived for the first time at a clear consciousness of their physical environment.. They saw with new eyes the vast disorder of their material surroundings, and began everywhere to try to bring shape and seemliness into the works which they themselves undertook. In all countries this new attitude showed itself most strikingly in the towns, but in England, since the governing classes had never so thoroughly as elsewhere divorced themselves from rural interests, it was also widely expressed in the countryside.

In the town the awakened consciousness led to a discovery of the most profound importance. Men now saw with a new understanding the collective basis of their city life, and they sought to express it in the physical form and association of their buildings. Beyond the jumble of their individual houses, beyond the twisted thoroughfares, beyond even the boldest conception they had hitherto had of their towns and their town life, they now found what was the quintessence of them all.

C

They discovered the Street.* They saw now that the street was not merely a necessary hole in the town. It was the town itself. And in discovering this they were discovering something of which those earlier civilizations from which they drew their inspiration had themselves but little conception. Herein the Renaissance was far more than a revival of past learning. It was an advance beyond anything that had yet been achieved.

One of the earliest references to the newly discovered importance of the Street, and one of the most striking indications of the impact of the Renaissance on the mind of an Englishman of the early sixteenth century is contained in Sir Thomas More's well-known description of his Utopia (1516).

"The stretes", More wrote of that imaginary town which was to be so different from the towns of sixteenth-century Europe,

the stretes be appointed and set furth very commodious and handsome, both for carriage, and also againste the windes. The houses be of faire and gorgious building, and on the strete side they stand joyned together in a long rowe through the whole strete without any partition or separation. . . . Their cronicles, even from the firste conquest of the Ilande, recorde and witnesse that the houses in the beginning were very low, and like homely cotages or poore sheppard houses, made at all adventures of everye rude pece of tymber, that came first to hande, with mudde walls, and ridged rooffes, thatched over with strawe. But now the houses be curiouslye buylded after a gorgious and gallante sorte, with three storyes one over another. The outsides of the walles be made either of harde flynte, or of plaster, or els of bricke, and the inner sydes be well strengthened with tymber work. The rooffes be plaine and flat, covered with a certen kinde of plaster that is of no coste, and yet so tempered that no fyre can hurt or perishe it.

Utopia remained a dream, but homes "buylded after gorgious and gallante sorte" eventually became the commonplace of every town in the kingdom. The discovery of the Street is generally accredited to mid-

*Barman: *Architecture.*

fifteenth-century Florence and other towns in northern Italy, but England holds an honourable place in its early development. In the courts and open quadrangles of the new colleges that were built at Oxford and Cambridge from the fifteenth century onwards, the possibility of the unified expression of buildings of many different units was developed in an unpretentious scale of quietness and easy formality that was to continue throughout its whole course to be the most delightful and notable characteristic of English civic design.

By a fortunate circumstance the full development of Renaissance ideals occurred at a time when England's growing prosperity afforded an unusual opportunity for their realization in the town: and though it can hardly be claimed that the opportunity was by any means fully exploited, at least it was not altogether neglected, as some of our towns bear witness to-day. By the middle of the seventeenth century England had outstripped all her rivals for the commercial leadership of Europe. London especially, with its population of 200,000 or more, had attained dominance, and was now the chief commercial city of the world. And the whole country was doubly in a stage of material consolidation. Town and village were in a continuous course of rebuilding, as well as of natural expansion, for by now wood was being almost universally discarded as the normal building material, and houses of brick and stone offered fashionable no less than physical advantages.

The first large-scale attempt at the formalization of the Street was designed by Inigo Jones, in the 1630's. Here in the very beginning was established that partnership of architect and enlightened landowner (in this case the Earl of Bedford) which during the next two hundred years gave to London, despite the lack of autocratic control which most other capital cities have had, that splendid series of related streets and squares which even to-day, ravished though they are, remain by far the most

39

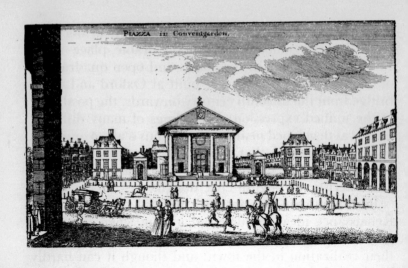

Covent Garden : from a 17th-century engraving.

extensive example of truly urbane building in any city of the world. "About the Centre of the Ground, he caused to be set out a large square or rather oblong piece of ground, 500 foot in Length and 400 in Breadth, and in this Plot of Ground, four large streets of about 50 or 60 foot Broad, have their entrance." Covent Garden Piazza, with its sides lined by formal arcaded buildings, was never completed in its full designed form; but it exerted an influence which, materialising slowly in Lincoln's Inn Fields, and Red Lion, Soho, Bloomsbury, and St. James's Squares towards the end of the century, established the domestic square in such public favour that it became almost a peculiarly English speciality and certainly the chief form of civic design in which a definite tradition was achieved in England. From the beginning of the eighteenth century onwards, square followed square in rapid succession until eventually London could boast of some hundreds of squares, as well as a multitude of harmonious streets, of a charm and refinement and a perfection of civic expression that neither Paris nor

40

Vienna nor any other of the boasted cities of the world can equal.

All this noble work (and a good deal more that was far from being noble) was in the nature of private development rather than town planning. Planning, which necessarily is the function of authority, would indeed have been remarkable for its absence had not authority itself been absent also. A plan like Wren's needs greater authority to enforce it than that of a city corporation packed with vested interests, or a committee of quibbling parish vestrymen. Yet, though the lack of positive action by authority was even more characteristic of seventeenth and eighteenth than it hitherto has been of twentieth-century London, there was nevertheless a restrictive control that was directed towards the promotion of the architectural unity of the town. As early as 1605 a royal proclamation required the forefronts of all houses to be of the uniform order decreed by the magistrates for the street in which they were situated, and provided that offenders against this decree should be brought before the Star Chamber. Another proclamation, of 1619, prohibited 'juteyes' or canting windows, and provided that, to secure some uniformity of treatment, shops were to have stone or brick pilasters in front, and that shop windows were to be arched. Again, in 1661, the King forbade the use of all projections save balconies; and six years later the Corporation decreed that 'the Breast-Summers of all houses do range of an equal height House with House.' How far these proclamations and decrees were enforced it is impossible to say, but their mere existence shows the fullness of the extent to which the essentially co-operative nature of street architecture was already realised.

It is natural that the influence of the Renaissance on the town should first be described as it affected London, for already in the sixteenth century London's continually expanding prosperity in the commercial field, as well as its importance as the seat of court and of government, was establishing it as by far the largest city in the country. The problem of its increasing size, indeed, became an obsession to its rulers throughout the seventeenth century, and dozens of royal proclamations, all equally vain, were passed to attempt to stop a growth which it was feared could only result in plagues and kindred catastrophes, and perhaps even in a challenge to the throne itself.

But it was in the new fashionable resorts that sprang into being through royal and aristocratic patronage, as well as in the metropolis, that the Street was carried to its perfection in England. In Bath, which, following a royal visit, suddenly developed into the earliest of fashionable watering places, a whole series of splendid streets was built from 1730 onwards, streets which in their boldness of conception and their refinement of detail were far beyond anything which had yet been achieved in England. Similarly throughout the whole course of the eighteenth century, and in the first decade or two of the nineteenth also, in Buxton, Cheltenham, Brighton, Weymouth, Ramsgate, Tenby and in a host of other resorts which followed upon the Georgian discovery of the pleasures of sea-bathing, town building was carried forward in that true Renaissance manner, growing ever more bland and urbane, where

> No single parts unequally surprise,
> All comes united to th' admiring eyes;
> No monstrous height, or breadth, or length appear;
> The whole at once is bold, and regular.

The civic consciousness reflected in nearly all these seventeenth and eighteenth-century town developments is remarkable indeed when we consider how slight was the civic control over the building activities during that period. The Regent Street and Regents Park development in London was the only large work that sprang

42

directly out of governmental initiative. The rest were the works of private landowners and speculating builders. These men did not undertake their work solely for the good of the community. They expected, and many of them got, considerable fortunes from it. But they were nevertheless imbued with civic ideals. They had a passion for 'improvement'—an operation which had not then acquired the sinister associations it has had in the recent past. The landowners, leasing off their building estates to developers, leased only to those who undertook to conform to designs that had been laid down with a sincere regard for beauty and seemliness. Even the speculating builders, right down from Dr. Nicholas Barbon to the Cubitts, considered the creation of new civic amenities a prime necessity of their operations, and for the achievement of this they were sometimes willing to sacrifice considerable profits, as witness the action of Grainger, the builder of those fine central streets which still to-day make Newcastle one of the most imposing of English provincial cities, who, because a recently-built theatre and a public market stood in the way of one of his new streets, rebuilt these on new sites at enormous cost to himself rather than divert his street and so impair the civic advantages of his work. And guiding and counselling these landowners and builders were their architects, who, from Inigo Jones and Wren to Nash, Pennethorne, Basevi and a crowd of others in London, from the Woods in Bath to Carr in Buxton, Dobson in Newcastle, Strahan in Bristol, Foulston in Plymouth, Papworth in Cheltenham and Burton in Brighton, were all of them inspired by a consciousness of their public responsibility as well as by a clear understanding of the civic nature of their technical problems—as witness again the actions of John Nash,* who spent £70,000 in buying up a house which blocked the north end of his Regent Street and threatened to destroy the whole

*Summerson: *John Nash*.

scheme, and who, again, because his Quadrant could only be successfully carried through as one undertaking, risked his fortune in building it himself rather than see his design muddled and botched, as it assuredly would have been if left to a number of individual hands.

These men, landowners, builders, architects, were all of them actual participants in the work. But over and above them were the people for whom the work was intended. It is upon these in the last resort that the responsibility must lie. These eighteenth-century towns-men recognised, as members of society, that conformity to certain rules of conduct is as necessary to the harmonious association of buildings as it is to men's. They knew that in conforming to these rules and in avoiding the public expression of their more flamboyant personal idiosyncrasies they were not surrendering their individuality and losing their souls. They were behaving as members of a civilised community, as citizens. They were expressing their civilization. Their buildings in association were indeed but an expression of their own personal good manners in their social relationships, of their sense of society, of their citizenship. To say all this may be to pile cliché upon platitude, but it is none the less true. And though in these days of uncertain values it may be a matter of mocking laughter, it is none the less true also that these streets and squares of this great period of English town development were the medium in which the boasted characteristics of English gentle-manliness were given their finest and most permanent expression.

By the time this English tradition of town building had come into its full flower towards the end of the eighteenth century, the towns reflected far more than this: they reflected, as indeed all towns must reflect, the civilization upon which they were founded. And the truest reflection was seen even more in the ordinary everyday towns than in the special places of metropolis

Stockton-on-Tees: from an 18th-century engraving.

and fashionable resort. It was particularly shown in the hundreds of small market towns up and down the country. These towns grew slowly, a public building here and there, a house or two, at most a short street. Most of their changed aspect came through rebuilding rather than new-building, and naturally that, too, was undertaken for single structures rather than for whole quarters at a time. Yet throughout the later part of the seventeenth and the whole of the eighteenth centuries the idea of the Street had so informed the national building tradition that, even in these slow accumulative growths and refurbishings, buildings generations apart in time stood together in a harmonious relationship of spirit that still gives the older parts of these towns a truer air of urbanity than have later places a hundred times as large. It is invidious to choose examples: anyone who has used his eyes to see can name them by the score.

45

Chichester, that exquisite though still insufficiently-admired small city, is perhaps the purest example still surviving. The older parts of King's Lynn, Farnham, Yarm, Lewes, Wisbech, Bewdley, Dorking, Taunton (with Blandford, differing from the rest in that it was rebuilt within a short period after being destroyed by fire) are all notable examples of the blandly urbane country towns of Renaissance England. But so are a hundred others. Towns like Preston, Stockton and Kidderminster still show glimpses of the pleasantness and refinement they had before they were brutalised and overwhelmed—as indeed does almost every town that existed before the first few decades of the nineteenth century. None of them, of course, had the full formal attributes of the continental Renaissance town. Few possessed even a vestige of the monumental design which many planners and architects even to-day believe to be the finest expression of town building. On the contrary they were almost entirely informal. Their splendours (if indeed they possessed any attributes that could be thus described) were almost as casual as those of the mediæval town. And they were as varied. They were varied not only in contrast with each other but in themselves. In spite of the harmonious relationship which their buildings displayed, the scenes that they made were warmly intimate, richly intricate, full of incident. In this they were different from the planned places, whose effects were broad and set. And it was not merely that they had incident of form; they were rich in incident of colour too, especially the towns of the south, where bright-painted façades contrasted with each other and with the red of brick, the grey of flint, the yellow of stone. These towns were lively yet harmonious, varied yet ordered, urbane yet unmannered, rich yet unostentatious, disciplined yet free.

These latter qualities were not, in the end, very different even where bolder Renaissance effects had been

46

aimed at. Even Bath, in spite of the monumentality of its parts, remained informal in its full effect. Even the London squares, regular though they were, made no deliberate grand sequences, aimed at no spectacular effects. Everywhere in spite of the formal relationship of many buildings to each other informality ensued in the large-scale result. The English Renaissance tradition of town building was not concerned with the grandiose schemes for creating architectural scenery such as were forced upon European towns by autocratic rulers. Here were no arrow-like roads slashing radial-wise through the town, no great avenues for monumental effect, no grand self-dramatising vistas, no squares built as scenery round royal monuments. The English tradition, being a genuine tradition arising naturally out of the lives and customs of the people, not being thrust upon them, was more intimately concerned with the life of the town and its citizens (or the more fortunate sections of them) than with spectacular displays of authority. It has been relegated to a lowly place in the history of civic design on that account. But most wrongly. Here in the domestic sphere the English had brought town building near to perfection. The house, the street and the town had been brought into a perfect synthesis. Street and square reflected the co-operative basis of the town, and yet in their charming domesticity they glorified (within the limits of the social values of the times) not Government nor Commerce nor Religion, but man himself, the Citizen. As the makers of towns the English of these generations were supreme in their contemporary world.

§

As the creators of landscape they had taken a still more individual line and had come even nearer to attaining perfection. And, moreover, whereas their urban achievements, though widespread enough, were still far from being general, their rural activities were on a scale and of a quality which can only be regarded as unparalleled in the history of civilization.

As in the town (though here a little later still), the full development of Renaissance ideals was not strongly felt until well into the seventeenth century. Inclosure had continued through Tudor times, though its extent was probably much exaggerated in contemporary writings. From the evidence of later years, it is certain that the greater part of the land was still cultivated on the common field system. It has been estimated that, from the middle of the fifteenth century to the beginning of the seventeenth, the areas inclosed amounted only to some two per cent. of the total area of the country. And this inclosure when it did take place did not necessarily mean *enclosure* into fields with hedges or fences (though sometimes it did), but rather absorption into large and undivided properties which often became the decorative country estates of prosperous merchants and wealthy townspeople.

The first influences of the Renaissance on landscape were seen in the garden. When the idea that a building or a series of buildings was something that could be consciously observed as a single design became established, the setting of its immediate surroundings became also a matter of some importance, and the formalization of the façade led towards the formalization of the garden, both in the shape and disposition of its layout and in that characteristic extravagance and contortion of topiary which we to-day particularly associate with the Tudors. This formalization was to be extended at a later time beyond the bounds of the garden into the countryside itself (particularly by means of that brilliant invention the ha-ha, or sunk fence), and it was thus that the conscious humanisation of the countryside began.

But if throughout this period inclosures from the lands occupied by the ancient agricultural economy were

48

small, the waste lands were continually shrinking (though some five-eighths of the country was still in a waste state in Tudor times). In the sixteenth and early seventeenth centuries the clearance of the forest part of the uncultivated area seems to have proceeded rapidly. By the middle of the seventeenth century, indeed, the destruction of timber had reached such alarming proportions, not only through forest clearance, but because of its use as ordinary fuel and for glass and iron furnaces and the like, that a general concern began to be felt that soon the existence of the British Navy itself would be imperilled by the scarcity of 'hearts of oak'. A survey of state forests in 1608 had recorded about 124,000 trees fit for the Navy; another survey in 1707 could report only some 12,500;* and towards the later part of the seventeenth century it could be said that all the estuaries and wide areas along the banks of every navigable river had been almost completely denuded of large timber.

Out of scarcity came forth riches, for it was this deplorable state of affairs that set going the movement which brought the English countryside out of its patchy universality into its rich and individual beauty. The man most keenly aware of the danger was John Evelyn, that curious-minded versatile man whose fame as a diarist has somewhat obscured his other claims to remembrance. In 1664 he published his *Sylva*, a book which was "a trumpet note of alarm to the nation on the condition of their woods and forests." Evelyn omitted no argument which might encourage his countrymen to practise the arts of arboriculture. Besides appealing to their patriotic feelings and their commercial instincts, he appealed also to their charity by demonstrating how the poor might benefit by planting on waste lands, and to their artistic sense by beseeching "Noble Persons to adorn their goodly Mansions and Demesnes with trees of venerable

*Stapledon: *The Land.*

49

shade." And he did so with such success that he could afterwards claim that he had induced landowners to plant many millions of trees.*

As Inigo Jones may be reckoned the founder of English civic design, so John Evelyn must be regarded as the father of the modern English landscape. His *Sylva* ran through many editions and was for generations the inspiration that led his countrymen towards a general practice of planting and rural adornment. Whereas the countryside had hitherto been regarded merely as the scene of economic activity, from now onward it was regarded also in the light of a pictorial composition whereon each man, working with Nature's own materials, might produce a scene of beauty for his descendants' future delight. It was a genuine æsthetic impulse. Here in England it was sought to create in actuality the ideal landscapes that Claude Lorraine, Salvator Rosa, Poussin and others had painted on canvas.

Of all the works ever undertaken in the history of civilization this surely was one of the noblest. It was a far nobler work even than that which displayed man's civilization in his cities. *That* work was performed for contemporary gain. Within a year or two of its initiation a building scheme could be raised into material fact. *This* work meant labour and expense with no hope of profit for the immediate undertakers of it. It would be at least half a century before the scene for which these trees were planted could begin to take its imagined shape: it would be a century or more before it could come to perfection. And even now when two and a half centuries have elapsed since first the work began to be undertaken we still enjoy what its initiators could never hope to see.

This new development in landscape did not, of course, gather its full strength immediately following Evelyn's

*Garner: *English Landed Interest.*

trumpet note. The opportunity for expressing it on any large scale was not yet available. For the common field system was still the basis of the country's agricultural economy. It is true that inclosure continued. Though there had been armed resistance against it at the beginning of the seventeenth century, and a number of Acts were directed towards its prevention, it still went on. The reclamation of the waste also continued, especially in the Fen district, where 100,000 acres of waterlogged wilderness were brought into cultivation through the works of the Dutchman, Vermuyden, who, on behalf of a Company of Adventurers headed by the Earl of Bedford, carried out the scheme which is still to-day the drainage system of the Bedford Level. But still at the end of the century these things had advanced so little that only half of the total area of the land was cultivated, and of this at least three-fifths was in the old open common fields.

The opportunity for the re-creation of the country-side came with the eighteenth century. It had by now become quite plain that the common field system had fallen out of gear and was hopelessly inefficient for the production of food for the rapidly increasing populations of both the towns and the countryside. Individuals held their land in narrow strips scattered wildly over all parts of a parish. The soil itself was sadly impoverished by the centuries of ploughing in the same direction which the narrowness of the various holdings had entailed; and in scores of other ways the thousand-year-old system now showed itself to be outworn. In addition to this the revolution that was taking place in agriculture itself also demanded a revolution in the methods of land tenure. The introduction of the drill, of new crops and new rotations, and the way in which the possibilities of these were handicapped by the working of strip culti-vation, all made the growing class of men who were interested in the improvement of the land and its out-

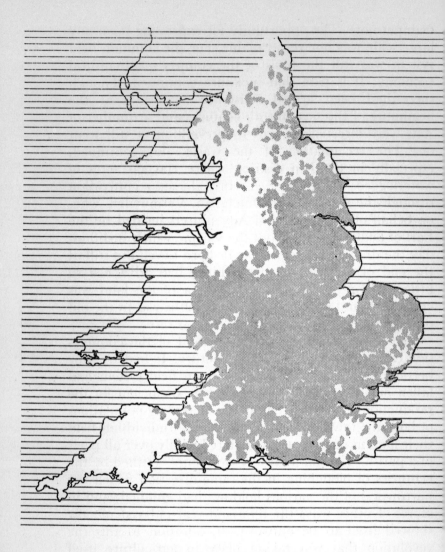

EXTENT OF THE OPEN FIELD SYSTEM IN ENGLAND
(based on a map in The Open Fields *by C. S. and C. S. Orwin)*

The shaded portions show the parishes where open fields have been traced or can be presumed ; and the map is a diagram of the geographical spread of the open fields, not a measure of their extent.   Much of the unshaded area covers mountain, moor, marsh and other uncultivable land.

put impatient to be rid of an agricultural economy which was now thought to be merely a barbarous survival of the dark ages. Thus the final abandonment of the common field system and the wholesale inclosure and redistribution of the land had become inevitable.

The old inclosure machinery had fallen out of date and was incapable of operation on the extensive scale that was now necessary. Fresh parliamentary power was therefore resorted to, and in 1701 the first of the modern Inclosure Acts was passed into law. In the course of the century some three and a half million acres of land, mostly common field, were inclosed under parliamentary powers: and there was besides a great though incalculable amount of inclosure and consolidation of properties through private treaties. It was these common field inclosures more than anything else that changed the appearance of the countryside.

The work entailed in the business of inclosure must have been of extraordinary complexity. First of all it was necessary for surveyors to measure and value every one of the innumerable small properties involved. Then the whole of the inclosure area was pieced out so that every holder received his proportionate share, with, as far as possible, each new holding laid out contiguous with the existing homestead. This often entailed a complete remodelling of the public road system, for while it was desirable that each new holding should be compact and unsevered by roads, it was also necessary that as far as possible it should have direct access to them. Hitherto the highways had been unfenced and unfixed: rights of passage only, which might deviate and alter to avoid obstacles and bad impassable patches. Now they became fixed narrow hedged strips which had to be fitted into the general pattern of the redistributed fields. So the winding sharp-turning and apparently erratic English country roads are not the result purely of ancient purposelessness and blind chance, but are a natural

D

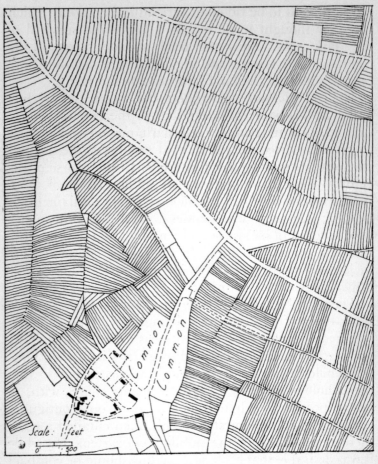

Scale: 1 feet

0' 500

The neighbourhood of the village of Balscott in the parish of Wroxton, Oxfordshire, in 1768, before inclosure. The firm lines represent, of course, the boundaries of plots, not hedges or other fences.

part of, and arose from, the individual development of English agriculture.

In the allocation of the new properties, the practice generally followed was to fix the lines of the fences so as to form square or rectangular enclosures. Each property was compulsorily enclosed by a fence, which was almost

54

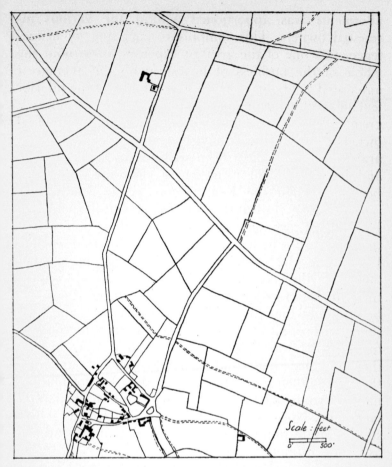

*The same area after inclosure (from a modern ordnance map). One or two
of the old division lines can still be traced: but here all the firm lines
represent hedges or other solid boundaries.*

invariably a quick hedge standing on a little ditched
bank in the lowland country, or a dry stone wall in the
hill country. The cost of 'public' fences alongside the road
was borne out of the general inclosure fund which was
assessed on each allotment in proportion to its size: and
the cost of the 'boundary' fences between the various

allotments was apportioned against the various interested owners. This compulsory enclosing by hedge-fences was one of the greatest expenses throughout the whole of the business of inclosure: on the average it amounted to about £1 an acre* (exlusive of the interior fencing within each allotment, of which there was a great deal, but which was the affair of the individual owners). It might easily have been dispensed with in the arable areas and have been replaced by some cheaper and less permanent form where enclosure was indispensable. Then the English countryside would have remained the universal countryside. But it persisted. It persisted not only for boundary definition within the inclosure schemes, but for private internal fencing. It became the common fencing in all the lowland parts of the country. And with it was coupled the planting of hedgerow trees. And although there can be no doubt that the planting of both hedges and trees (and the leaving of selected self-sown trees to come to full growth) was largely a utilitarian activity in that they provided shade and shelter as well as boundaries, they were much more than merely this. Not for nothing had Evelyn invoked his countrymen to adorn the natural landscape. Now that the opportunity had come it was still his inspiration that led them to utilise it for aesthetic as well as economic improvement.

The impulse that Evelyn had inspired sprang indeed into full strength at this time. Every landlord, whether he was involved in inclosure schemes or not, became an enthusiastic practitioner of landscape art; and Jane Austen's Henry Crawford and Peacock's Mr. Milestone represented only two of numerous widely differing types of enthusiastic 'improvers'. Infinite discussion and vast sums of money were expended on this art which every man could practise. So at the very time when Cowper was speaking of the 'God-made country', the English

*Garner: *English Landed Interest.*

56

countryside was being consciously humanised with tireless energy and admirable imagination.

The first results of Evelyn's appeal had been an attempt to formalize the landscape in the continental manner. In the late seventeenth and early eighteenth centuries the chief method of rural adornment had been the planting of chestnut, elm and beech in great avenues that ran through miles of country and then petered out ignominiously in a ditch or a bog, or merely ceased in an abrupt confession of futility. But the invincible undulation of the English landscape and the growing appreciation of natural beauty had defeated this: and now the activities of the landscapists became founded on a realization and acceptance of natural informality, and were governed by the desirability of enhancing this rather than of attempting to destroy it. The chief of the professional practitioners of this 'landscape planting' were Kent and Capability Brown, and after them, Repton. These men have been much blamed, and rightly, for some of their practices. But despite the mishandling and misapplication to which they were afterwards subjected, it was the theories which these men and a thousand others applied that moulded the English rural scene into the lovely pattern of its recent perfection.

It was to the enormous parks of the great landowners that the most intensive landscaping activity was directed. Here indeed an entirely new type of scenery may be said to have been achieved. But the smaller landowners, the local squires, the yeoman farmers even, were not to be damped in their enthusiasm for improvement because their lands were merely fields instead of parks. They could follow Addison's advice to "make a pretty landskip" of their own possessions by planting trees in their hedgerows—which they did with great enthusiasm. And for this, particularly, the eighteenth century should be blessed; for it is the single-standing or small-grouped hedgerow trees, far more than the park-lands and the woods and copses, which give the English scene its park-like quality, its intimacy and that delight which arises from the association of beauty with ordinary everyday things.

Horace Walpole's encomium on William Kent (*History of Modern Taste in Gardening*, 1785) reflects so accurately the enthusiasm that was aroused by the new art of landscape 'improvement' that, familiar though it is, it is worth quoting again at some length:

At that moment appeared Kent, painter enough to taste the charm of landscape, bold and opinionative to dare and to dictate, and born with a genius to strike out a great system from the twilight of imperfect essays. He leaped the fence and saw that all nature was a garden. He felt the delicious contrast of hill and valley changing imperceptibly into each other, tasted the beauty of the gentle swell or concave scoop, and remarked how loose groves crowned an easy eminence with happy ornament . . . The pencil of his imagination bestowed all the arts of landscape on the scenes he handled. The great principles on which he worked were perspective, and light and shade. Groups of trees broke too uniform or too extensive a lawn: evergreens and woods were opposed to the glare of the champaign . . . Thus selecting favourite objects and veiling deformities by screens of plantation, sometimes allowing the rudest waste to add its foil to the richest theatre, he realised the compositions of the greatest masters in painting. Dealing in none but the colours of Nature and catching its most favourable features, men saw a new creation opening before their eyes. The living landscape was chastened or polished, not transformed. Freedom was unrestricted, and where any eminent Oak, or Master Beech, had escaped maiming and survived the forest, bush and bramble was removed and all its honours were restored to distinguish and shade the plain. Where the united plumage of an ancient wood extended wide its undulating canopy, and stood venerable in its darkness, Kent thinned the foremost ranks and left but so many detached and scattered trees as softened the approach of gloom and blended a chequered light with the thus lengthened shadows of the remaining columns. So many men of all ranks devoted themselves to the new improvements that it is surprising how much beauty has been struck out, with how few absurdities. In the meantime, how rich, how gay, how picturesque the face of the country! Every journey is made through a succession of pictures; and even where taste is wanting

William Shenstone's ' garden ' at The Leasowes, made in 1745.

in the spot improved, the general view is embellished by variety. If no lapse to barbarism, formality and seclusion is made, what landscapes will dignify every quarter of our island when the daily plantations that are making have attained venerable maturity!

Since we have been familiarized to the study of landscape (Walpole concludes), we hear less of what delighted our sportsmen ancestors, a fine open country. Wiltshire, Dorsetshire and such ocean-like extents, were formerly preferred to the rich blue prospects of Kent, to the Thames-watered view in Berkshire, and to the magnificent scale of Nature in Yorkshire. An open country is but a canvas on which a landscape might be designed. (And a previous footnote describing a particular landscape effect leaves no doubt as to from whom the pictorial inspiration of these Georgian landscapists was derived: "Extensive lawns, richly enclosed by venerable beech woods, and chequered by single beeches of vast size . . . recall such exact pictures of Claude Lorraine, that it is difficult to conceive that he did not paint them from this very spot.")

No such great æsthetic impulse to rural adornment as this has occurred at any time anywhere else in the world. It was indeed a remarkable manifestation of civilization. And it was not limited to the planting of trees and suchlike use of natural objects. It extended also to purely artificial creations, and governed the building of houses no less than the making of parks. Thus probably the majority of country houses were rebuilt at this time, and in their rebuilding they were sited with as close a regard for landscape as for architectural effect. Thus also were large parts of many of the existing villages swept away and reconstructed in the consuming passion for 'improvement' which seems to have beset everyone. Most of this work was no doubt but an early kind of private 'slum clearance', with rehousing taking place on the same site. But some villages, at least, were bodily transplanted to another place for the sake of landscape effect, as were Lowther, Milton Abbas, Coneysthorpe and Harewood, for example, all of whose forerunners had been situated too close to manorial windows for aristocratic comfort.

In all this rebuilding, the men of the eighteenth and early nineteenth century showed the admirable balance of their outlook and the wide range of their understanding. For men who were engaged in dealing with so romantic a business as creating landscape it would seem to us to-day to have been an extraordinarily difficult thing not to have lapsed either into the romantic in architecture or into formality in planting. But they did neither in excess. Creating a landscape and building a mansion or a cottage were for them different though sympathetic activities each with its own separate æsthetic controlling principles. And rarely did they let those principles get confused. They understood the value of contrast. They knew that the inherent qualities of different objects are best expressed in their own terms. So they knew no fear in dealing frankly with a purely artificial object in the midst of natural objects. Nor was there any reason why their new villages or their additions to older villages should be other than normal contemporary buildings. So villages like Tremadoc, Harewood, Blanchland, and a score of others, were built in their wild or gentle surroundings with a conscious though loose formality; and the new houses that rose in the old streets of all the ten thousand villages of England displayed in their façades the same urbane characteristics as did their counterparts in the country town or the capital city.

The new buildings on the outskirts of the towns were, of course, the same kind. The London squares, though we regard them to-day as essentially central-city in their character, were originally built in the open fields. But that was no reason to eighteenth-century builders why they should not be of an utterly urban quality. These men knew no such thing as a suburb in the modern meaning of the word, a bastard form half-way between town and country. A suburb was on the outskirts of the town, but still it was *of* the town, proudly and sheerly urban.

And here indeed is the crux of the matter. The towns of eighteenth-century England were by no means divorced from the countryside. The majority of the population, indeed, still lived there. The countrymen themselves marketed their produce in the town: the most powerful of the citizens of the town were deeply involved in the life of the countryside. Yet all these people recognised the essential difference in form of these two essential parts of the national synthesis. So highly had they developed their consciousness of their visible environment, so deep did their understanding go of the essential qualities of each part of the physical scene, that without confusion or hesitation, with an apparent ease that in no way reflects the magnificence of their achievement, these few generations of Englishmen created at one and the same time a countryside that is unique in the history of the world, and a series of towns and villages that have never been surpassed for that quiet domestic grace and beauty which is the true expression of citizenship and civilization.

CHAPTER FOUR

HELL, UTOPIA, AND MIDDLESBROUGH

IT IS A SADDENING FACT that, having extolled the achievements of almost any period of history, one must immediately proceed to qualify and excuse. We may rightly say that the seventeenth and eighteenth centuries were the golden age of landscape and civic design in England. But having said that it is necessary to remember that gold is notoriously a metal of limited circulation, and that while its shining splendour may have gleamed in the building and scenic transactions of the fortunate few, the majority of the people had as usual to be content with a much baser metal.

The inclosures which had offered such opportunity for landscape improvement brought anything but improvement to a large section of the inhabitants of that landscape. When the pattern of hedges was applied to the commons, the open fields and the waste, it made them pictorially friendly; but it was a friendliness which the peasants, shut out by those very hedges from lands where they had immemorially held rights of pasturage, could hardly be expected to enjoy. The inclosures, indeed, were carried through at the expense of a crying injustice to the poor, and they were carried through not only for the æsthetic satisfaction but for the enormous financial benefit of the richer classes. Even Arthur Young, the chief advocate of inclosure, had to admit, in 1801, that nineteen out of twenty Inclosure Acts had wronged the poor. The bitterness of the feeling over this

62

wrong may still be felt in the well-known jingle of the times:

> The law doth punish man or woman
> That steals the goose from off the common,
> But lets the greater felon loose
> Who steals the common from the goose.

The same nice distinctions in social values were reflected in the old and new towns in all parts of the country. The glories of Bath and Cheltenham were not to be seen in the quarters inhabited by the less fashionable members of the community. Behind the pleasant façades of the houses of the gentry and the more prosperous merchants which lined the main streets of the country towns, out of sight beyond the narrow archways that gave the dead-end alleys and wyndes access to the main street, the 'lower orders of society' were congregated in crowding and crowded cottages. In London there had been other building than that of fine streets and fashionable squares, and the old houses that were deserted for those new ones in Bloomsbury and the West End remained to become the teeming rookeries of the poor.

Further, even in the best of the new developments the perfection of the architecture of the Street was not accompanied by the perfection of that less inspiring but none the less necessary art, the regulation of its sanitation. Water supply was still indifferent in the best of places: the disposal of sewage and refuse was carried out, if at all, by the most primitive of methods. Even the cleansing and repair of the public streets was so unorganised that as late as 1761 every man was responsible for removing the dirt and repairing the pavement in front of his own door. In all these things there was still little or no realization of the necessity of co-operative action. It was all too rarely that a corporation considered it necessary to appoint an expert to report on 'The Paving, Lighting and Draining of the Town', as did the governors of Abergavenny when they commissioned John Nash to do so in 1793. Yet important though these things undoubtedly are it is as easy to over-emphasize as to under-emphasize their effect on the pleasantness of the Georgian town.

For one thing the towns were still small, and their association with the countryside was very real. London was far away the largest city; yet the fields were still within so close reach of almost every part of it that even towards the end of the eighteenth century a writer could complain of the outskirts of Westminster that they were invaded on Sundays by "dirty blackguards, and poor parentless children, who have not any friends to take care of them, going about the fields and ditches where wild honey-suckles, nettles, and thistles grow, with bottles and catching of bees, wasps, ladybirds, blue-bottles and other winged insects".* Bristol, with 100,000 inhabitants, was still easily the second town in England. For the rest, the greater part of even the flourishing places contained only from two to four thousand people, and away beyond their boundaries stretched not only fields and orchards but sometimes extensive commons that were available for sport and pleasure. So that, bad as conditions often were, it was only later, when the small hand-working towns were turned through the advent of steam power and the growth of the factory system into mass-working industrial towns with greatly increased populations, that sanitary questions and the general problems of town organisation became, as they rapidly did become, desperately urgent.

It was the overwhelming increase of working-class population, reacting on the ill-balanced social code, that caused the disaster. How the growing needs of the machine could immediately result in an increase in the fertility of its slaves is still something of a mystery, though it is undoubtedly true that a low standard of life stimulates the growth of population. There can be

*George: *Town Life* (in *Johnson's England*).

64

no doubt that the standard of living which the new factory system imposed upon the hordes of workers it absorbed (among them a great body of peasantry disinherited through inclosure) was inhumanly low. So there came within a period of a few decades a complete transformation of the map of England.

It was not only that the population increased at an amazing rate. Its new distribution was equally striking. In 1700 the most populous counties had been Middlesex, Somerset, Gloucester, Wiltshire and Northampton.* In 1800 only Middlesex, with London accounting for most of its population, remained on this list. Lancashire, West Riding, Staffordshire and Warwickshire had all leaped beyond the others even thus early in the new industrial dispensation. How that happened, how the incidence of the new industrialism fell as it did so that certain industries which had hitherto flourished in the south migrated northwards, as iron working migrated from Sussex to the coalfields, and as woollen manufacture became centralised in Yorkshire through the inadaptability of the southern manufacturers to new conditions, it is no part of our business here to describe. But one point about it is worthy of notice, for it has had its effect on the whole subsequent course of English social history. Henceforward England became almost two countries. The Midlands and the North advanced grimly along a hideous road of industrialism, while the South (in which, significantly, was situated the capital city) slumbered fitfully in the tree-folded parks and the half-dead small towns and villages of its 'improved' landscape.

Some idea of the rapidity of the growth of the new manufacturing towns may be gained from the following instances. In 1801 Liverpool had a population of 77,000; in 1821 it had 118,000; by 1841 it had some 300,000. Manchester had 95,000 inhabitants in 1801; in 1821 it had

*Hammond: *The Town Labourer.*

65

238,000. In 1801 Leeds had 60,000, Sheffield 45,000, Birmingham 73,000; by 1821 they had 123,000, 91,000, and 146,000 respectively, all having grown by 100 per cent. or more in twenty years. And while the growth of the existing towns was of this spectacular kind the sudden upshooting of new towns where before had been virgin fields, or at most a hamlet of a few houses, was even more remarkable. Parishes which for centuries had housed but a few score people, in a space of a few years could count their ten thousand. As the workers flocked into them, English and Welsh, Irish from the distressed districts, Highlanders from the depopulated glens, the towns sprang up at a nightmare rate and of a nightmare character. Fastest of all grew the cotton towns; the iron towns, the pottery towns, the woollen towns, followed hardly less swiftly; while all about the coalfields gaunt mining villages grew side by side with fiery waste heaps in the very shadow of the pitheads, often enough in the pit yards themselves.

In the feverish activity and the intoxication of dreams of wealth that all this change entailed, what were the influences of that so recent golden age of town development? A tradition that has been gathering strength and maturity for two hundred years, however limited it may be in its application, can hardly go by the board in the space of a decade or two. Nor did it. For well into the middle of the century, in the west-end developments in London, in the health resorts, and in one remarkable instance in an industrial city (Newcastle 1830-40), the tradition was maintained with splendid effect. And though, as has been shown, working-class houses had never been brought within the scope of civic design, at least they continued to share to a considerable degree the common building tradition, so that most of even the early slum streets were architecturally, if not hygienically, decent.

In one respect the speed with which the new industrial

66

Newcastle-on-Tyne, 1850.

towns grew should have assisted in the establishment of careful planning, for where before, in all except the quickly-growing fashionable resorts, the slow accumulative growth of a house here and a cottage there had made organised growth difficult, now the necessity of building whole streets at a time demanded, of itself, a plan of some sort or other. The result was, of course, bound to be affected by what determined the plan. And what did determine the plan, the social values of the time being what they were, was the cost of land. It has been said that in parts of Lancashire the rent of land was increased through the development of the factory system by as much as 3000 per cent. in the course of a few years.* So, money being a consideration above all others, the sensible method of building new towns was to build them as tightly and as inexpensively as possible.

And tightly and cheaply they were built. The problem

*Hammond: *The Town Labourer.*

resolved itself into the simple terms of the greatest possible number of the smallest possible houses on the least possible space. So the new town grew progressively more solid as the mad scramble for wealth and production quickened towards its mid-century climax of brutality, until eventually, as in the back-to-back houses and in the crammed courts and alleyways, the town consisted solely of buildings and the means of access to them.

Added to all this was an intensification of that neglect of sanitary organisation which had always hitherto characterized men's urban association. This was the most dreadful feature of all. The new townsmen breathed and drank each other's filth and the filth of their factories. Modern imagination boggles at the outrageous horror of the common conditions of that time. But since it is easy to fall into unfairness as well as into perhaps inaccurate generalization in applying the standards of to-day to these conditions of a hundred years ago, it may be as well to quote briefly one or two descriptions of contemporary observers of that awful progression to darkness.

Here, then, is Friedrich Engels's well-known sketch of an urban prospect in the Manchester of 1844:

In a rather deep hole, in a curve of the Medlock, and surrounded on all sides by tall factories and high embankments covered with buildings, stand two groups of about two hundred cottages, built chiefly back-to-back, in which live about two thousand human beings, most of them Irish. The cottages are old, dirty, and of the smallest sort, the streets uneven, fallen into ruts and in part without drains or pavements; masses of refuse, offal and sickening filth lie among standing pools in all directions; the atmosphere is poisoned by the effluvia from these, and laden and darkened by the smoke of a dozen tall factory chimneys. A horde of ragged women and children swarm about here, as filthy as the swine that thrive upon the garbage heaps and in the puddles . . . In the whole region, for each one hundred and twenty persons, one usually inaccessible privy is provided.

Here, again, is Nassau Senior, about the same time, describing new settlements around the same city:

These towns, for in extent and number of inhabitants they are towns, have been erected with the utmost disregard of everything except the immediate advantage of the speculating builder (how familiar a ring it still has!). In one place we found a whole street following a ditch because in this way cellars could be secured without the cost of digging . . . Not one house of this street escaped the cholera.

Or, again, here are the results of a survey made in Leeds in the 1830's. Out of 568 streets examined, only 68 were paved. Whole streets floated with sewage, and one of these, with 176 families in it, had not been cleaned for 15 years. In these 568 streets there were 451 public houses, 98 brothels, 2 churches and 39 meeting houses.* In Bristol, out of 3,000 houses examined, 1,300 were without water. In Manchester one family in ten, in Liverpool one family in every five, lived in a cellar. And so the tale could go on over the whole country, south as well as north, in old expanding city as well as in new upstart town.

If the pre-Renaissance town can still be occasionally glimpsed in corners of a few of our cathedral cities, these early Victorian towns can more readily be seen; for they are still the places where a large proportion of the working-class of twentieth-century England must live. As parts of the later towns and cities that have since grown around them, they have been tidied up and much improved. They have been sewered; their roads have been paved. But the genuine article in almost all its original impurity may still be sampled in hundreds of company-built colliery villages in any of the older coalfields. There the gaunt, gardenless, even yardless rows face back and front on to roads still unpaved after

*Mottram: *Town Life* (in *Early Victorian England*).

Pugin's Contrasts: a Catholic town in 1440.

town as a focus of a civilization, a centre where the emancipating
and enlightening influences of the time can act with rapidity and
with effect, the school of the social arts, the nursery of social enterprise, the witness to the beauty and order and freedom that men
can bring into their lives, had vanished from all minds.

Not quite from all minds, fortunately. Not all were
blinded in this scramble for the glittering prizes of
expanding markets. A few saw the shameful horror of it.
But if the glitter blinded the rest, the horror blinded
most of these. What, for instance, did the architects do—
those immediate inheritors of that great tradition which
had been so recently overthrown? Did they rise up and
attempt to re-establish the tradition, to broaden it and
bring within its influence all this vast activity in a sphere
which had been so long ignored? They did not. Seduced
by romanticism, they hated the tradition as much as
the chaos that had succeeded it. Instead, they drew
themselves apart, and, extolling the glories not of the
recent but of the remote past, they fled, as the younger
Pugin fled, crying out against the gasworks, the railways,
the foundries and all the rest of the instruments of the

Pugin's Contrasts: the same town in 1840.

horrible present, to find refuge in a dream of Gothic spires rising above a world unsullied by hard and bitter realities.

In contrast to this flight of the technicians into the past a few courageous prophets gazed into the future. One or two did more even than that; they set about them to show what might be done immediately. Thus Robert Owen, that early practical Socialist, after producing in 1816 a plan for the establishment of small self-contained industrial-agricultural communities at intervals throughout the countryside, himself attempted to develop a model industrial town at Orbiston near Motherwell (1820). Much later, in 1852, one Titus Salt planned and built a reasonably civilized village around his factory at Saltaire near Bradford. But most interesting of all was a plan suggested and worked out in great detail by that curious man, James Silk Buckingham, in his book, *National Evils and Practical Remedies* (1848).

The objects chiefly kept in view (he wrote of Victoria, his Associated Temperance Community) have been to unite the greatest

73

degree of order, symmetry, space and healthfulness, in the largest supply of air and light, and in the most perfect system of drainage, with the comfort and convenience of all classes: the one proportion of accommodation to the probable numbers and circumstances of various ranks; ready accessibility to all parts of the town under continuous shelter from sun and rain when necessary: with the disposition of public buildings in such localities as to make them easy of approach from all quarters, and surrounded with space for numerous avenues of entrance and exit. And in addition to all these a large admixture of grass lawn, garden ground, and flowers, and an abundant supply of water—the whole to be united with an elegance and economy as may be found practicable.

Here was a prophet indeed for 1848. No escapist, this. Victoria was to be a town of here and now, not an impossible re-creation of some dim mediæval dream. All the most recent advances in science and technology were to be utilized in its creation. The time was the age of iron? Very well: the entire town will be built of iron. An age of smoke and darkness? There will be no smoke in this town, for special appliances will prevent it, or where unpreventable will consume it. Nor shall this be any city of dreadful night. One enormous light on a thirty-foot tower in the centre will illuminate the entire place. Nor will it ever grow vast and ungainly. While it shall have every form of building and equipment to facilitate a full community life, its size will be limited. Beyond the factories outside the town, beyond the green belt of open country surrounding it, "smaller offspring might be formed, fostered and assisted by the Parent Town from which they spring". Brave Buckingham! His plans came to naught, but his was indeed a remarkable vision in that age of darkness and despair.

Victoria might remain for ever an unrealised ideal, but the reform of the hell that the English towns had now become could not much longer be delayed. To put any measure of reform into operation, however, there had to be some efficient means of local government. And that was precisely what the towns had not got. In the 1830's, London (outside the city) was administered by no fewer than 300 bodies consisting of 10,500 persons (many of whom were self-elected) working under 240 Acts.* Manchester, a community of over 200,000 people, was governed by the Lord of the Manor—who lived some thirty or forty miles away in Staffordshire. Most of the new towns were in the same position. It was clear that something had to be done about it. So in 1835 a Municipal Corporation Act was passed which gave the towns that democratic government through which they are organised to-day.

Once the organisation of this local basis of government was established the story of the towns henceforward became bound up with the slow acquisition, mostly from reluctant Parliaments, of the powers necessary to make that organisation successful. This is not the place to recount the development of local government. We are much more concerned with its results. And though in many ways that government has been most admirably successful, the physical form and appearance of our towns to-day bear witness to the depths of its failure in others.

Since local government itself first arose out of those conditions of insanitation which have been described, so throughout the whole of the remainder of the nineteenth century it was directed almost solely towards the improvement of those conditions and their avoidance in new developments. The enormous extensions of the existing towns, and the still further new towns which continued to grow at a wild-fire rate to house the ever-accelerating increase of population, were controlled by a succession of Public Health Acts culminating in that one of 1875 which is still regarded as the charter of the modern town. After three-quarters of a century the awful nightmare was over. Streets were paved; filth was taken away in sewers. Water was 'laid on'. Every family had an inalienable right to a certain minimum of light

*Mottram: *Town Life* (in *Early Victorian England*).

air. The Camp was cleaned up—but it still remained a Camp.

For if the nightmare was past, the awakening that succeeded it was of a most depressing dreariness. The town might no longer be foul but it was dead flat. It was also very stale, though by no means unprofitable. Restrictive hygiene had produced a dull sterility which the swollen bodies of the ever-expanding cities made all the more fearful to contemplate.

It is useless to attempt to recount the progress of this all-pervading dullness. Even horror has its story. Dullness has none. Year after year the towns developed, continually thrusting outwards, coalescing, many of them, into vast unescapable deserts of arid brick. Houses, factories, railways tangled together into a shapeless characterless mass, without plan, without cohesion, unquickened by any quality of pride, untouched by any spark of imaginative design. Still more houses; still more factories. Here a small sooty park 'landscaped' to a most touching incongruity. Here an extremely Gothic Town Hall; there a no less Gothic sewage farm. Still more houses and then again still more. Dreariness, drabness, dullness—the sanitary Victorian town.

It was all inevitably exemplified in the Street. If at the end of the eighteenth century the Street had been brought near to perfection, here at the end of the nineteenth, in that awful creation contemptuously known as the 'Byelaw Street', it was brought to the final limits of degradation. Where before street and square had been the pattern to which buildings subscribed in their co-operative association, the pattern within which the design of the various units had been subordinated to the design of the whole for the glory of the town, the Street had now become but a row of mean featureless cells that were closely associated for no other reason than that economy demanded it. The earlier uniformity had been that willingly adopted for social harmony by a

76

body free of agents conscious of their independence and power. Now the pattern was unmistakably that of a uniform thrust forcibly upon an undifferentiated mob of human ciphers. No longer did even a small part of the town glorify man, the Citizen, He was of no account in his own place. Nothing was glorified. Not even industry. Within a hundred years the nation that had once seemed likely to build the finest was building the foulest towns the civilized world has known.

Now indeed the town had lost in men's eyes its proud place as a symbol of their civilization, as "the school of the social arts, the nursery of social enterprise, the witness of the beauty and order and freedom that men can bring into their lives". It was none of these things. It was a dark prison from which they longed to escape, if only some means of escape were possible. Now indeed the Street had lost all possibility of beauty in the very country that had once brought it to perfection. In only too terrible truth was it the quintessence of the town. It symbolised the hopelessness, the dreariness, the degradation, the repression, the cold and squalid monotony of contemporary urban life. The town might have to remain, in economic necessity. But the Street, the symbol of its tyranny, was doomed.

CHAPTER FIVE

UNIVERSAL SUBURBIA

IT WOULD BE EASY to attribute the sole responsibility for the condition of the Victorian town to the
social upheaval caused by the Industrial Revolution.
The evil of the mid-century developments, which must
be laid mainly upon that cataclysm, makes such an
attribution natural. Yet the explanation is surely too
simple which attributes to the desire for profits and to
social irresponsibility the whole long decline throughout
the greater part of the century. The decline of architecture, that art which is so large a part of civic design,
cannot, for instance, be explained away in these simple
terms. That decline arose out of a change and a confusion in æsthetic ideals. And so inevitably did some
part at least of the failure of civic design itself.

It has already been shown how the idea of the Street,
and through that a new conception of the town, arose
out of that change in man's attitude towards his environment, that awakening desire to bring the material world
into a satisfying human relationship, which was brought
about by the Renaissance. Under that impulse architects
and builders had cast off the traditions which had
developed down the previous centuries, deeming them
incapable of bringing about the ordered beauty which
they found alone to be satisfactory ; and they had
established in their place a reasoned technique which
with unfaltering faith they developed through a course
of two centuries to that culmination which gave us the
eighteenth-century town. Under the same kind of
impulse and with the same faith the landowners and

78

their advisers had performed the even greater work of bringing a new beauty and order to the countryside. But maturity seems always to have in itself the seeds of its own destruction; and, by the time the Renaissance philosophy of humanism was being given its most triumphant physical expression, the very spirit which had created it, that direct enquiring attitude of mind, had so extended men's knowledge and understanding that the clear vision became blurred, the serene confidence shaken, the fine singleness of purpose dissipated by a host of distracting interests and doubt-engendering influences. Thus eighteenth-century antiquaries familiarizing mediæval art and institutions which had hitherto been deemed merely barbarous, and eighteenth-century scientists explaining the mysteries of Nature, and poets softening with a seductive web of words her hitherto overwhelming austerities, had created that Romantic Revival which struck deep at the very roots of their own civilization.

It struck first of all at their expression of that civilization in the countryside. When an object of awe has had its causes and character explained away it is apt, if it is an inanimate object at any rate, to lose much of its capacity for inspiring terror. So when the existence of such natural phenomena as mountains could be scientifically accounted for, and particularly at a time when through men's own activity the wild natural scene had been so tamed and reduced as to leave only a few obstinate patches of chaos standing out in contrast to the familiar and friendly shape of the everyday world— when this had happened, men, almost it would seem in their sheer perversity, began to be drawn away in their sympathies from the scenes which had recently been created with so much devotion, to surrender themselves, in an abjectness of worship, to the fascination of the wild and the untamable.

Up to the last two or three decades of the eighteenth

century, that is up to the greatest appreciation of and the widest practice in humanised landscape, mountains and moors had been regarded as unsightly and worse than useless excrescences upon the earth's surface. Dr. Johnson in his *Journey to the Western Isles* (1775) could say of the Scottish Highlands that "an eye accustomed to flowery pastures and waving harvests is astonished and repelled by this wide extent of hopeless sterility". In his opinion Johnson was giving no mere exhibition of his conservative and cantankerous nature. He was expressing what was, and always had been, the general attitude towards wild country. It was only because of this attitude, indeed, that men had ever set about improving the natural scene and reducing it to order and intimacy. And yet, by the time that order had been fully achieved, at the very time of its coming to perfection, men's scale of values had so changed that it was soon possible for a man like Ruskin to declare categorically that "mountains are the beginning and the end of all natural scenery".

This was indeed a remarkable change of attitude. Fortunately it had little immediate result in the rural scene. Its main result was to come later; and in the meantime there was little new work to be undertaken in the countryside. It is true that in the coalfields, and in other parts where geological conditions offered a suitable field for commercial exploitation, patches of landscape were reduced to a desolation of burning waste-heaps and poisoned stagnant marsh. It is true also that the railways which followed the invention of the steam locomotive imposed an occasional harshness of line upon the flowing curves of the landscape pattern (and it was in this connection that the change of values was first well illustrated, for what little opposition was made to scenic destruction by the railways was more or less limited to mountain districts, as when Wordsworth successfully resisted the projected Windermere-Keswick line in 1844, and Ruskin unsuccessfully indulged in his magnificent rhetorical protest against the line from Bakewell to Buxton). In addition to these non-agricultural activities, inclosure continued for well on into the century. In the first forty years or so some two million acres, chiefly moor and fen, were brought into cultivation, and after that a further 600,000 acres, chiefly this time from manorial commons, were inclosed before, in 1869, the whole movement was brought to a sudden and too-long-delayed end by the London Corporation's successful battle against the inclosure of Epping Forest.

But all these activities were limited in scale and scope, and for much the greater part of the English countryside the nineteenth century was a period of the slow maturing of the eighteenth-century plantings. Some further planting for sporting purposes was undertaken; more foreign trees, including new varieties of conifers (and a far more widespread use of that species), were introduced; and gradually as a result of the repeal of the Corn Laws a greater acreage of land was laid down to permanent grass. For the rest, the scenes that the eighteenth-century landscapists had planned developed slowly to the perfection of maturity, mellowed to a rich warm beauty till the country side took on the appearance of a vast tree-folded park—all to the indifference or at most the merely casual interest of a people so seduced by romanticism that they actually preferred the barbarous to the humanised, preferred mountain and moor to the scenes of man-created beauty.

The Romantic Revival, however, if it did not immediately affect the already organised rural scene, had a more noticeable effect upon the town. The renewal of interest in Gothic architecture as well as the new-found delights of informality in natural attributes led inevitably towards the destruction of so formal a creation as the Renaissance Street. Shortly after the turn of the century the beginnings of the reaction against Renaissance formality were already to be observed in occasional excursions into romantic expression by architects who normally worked in the old tradition. Thus Nash could design the 'villages' in Regent's Park (1824), as well as Regent Street and the rest of his admirably civic developments. Thus, too, could Decimus Burton build, in the neighbourhood of his own fine Calverly Promenade at Tunbridge Wells, a whole estate of detached and semi-detached villas (1828). Here were instances, and there were many others, of a turning away from the Street long before it became debased through unsympathetic handling and social callousness.

These early excursions from the Renaissance town were little more than experiments with a new aesthetic formula. It was not long, however, before they were prompted by other motives and were given far weightier justification. Under the guidance of Ruskin, moral indignation was added to aesthetic dissatisfaction to further the breakaway from the formal Street. As the principal object of his indignation, Ruskin chose Edinburgh New Town (though it might equally have been Bath or Bloomsbury); and so great did his obsession with that place become that throughout a considerable portion of his long life he lost no opportunity of fulminating against it and all that it stood for. Even he had to grant that it had some attraction. "As far as I am acquainted with modern architecture," he admitted, "I am aware of no streets which in simplicity and manliness of style or general breadth and brightness of effect equal those of the New Town at Edinburgh." Yet for him the "rudeness" of the Cannongate was infinitely to be preferred to the New Town's "dullness, its deathful formality of street." He was revolted to the very soul to find that in Queen Street there were "six hundred and seventy-eight windows, absolutely similar and altogether devoid of relief by decoration." For such crimes, while he "would like to destroy and rebuild the East End of

London", he would, he said, "destroy *without rebuilding* the New Town of Edinburgh."

But there was still another change that militated against the continuance of the old urban tradition. For this was the age not only of Romance but of *Laissez-faire*, of the individual-over-all—of the successful individual, that is. So the Street became doubly damned. Co-operation? When all-alone-I-did-it? To that the new towns and suburbs, which towards the middle of the century the railways made possible for the wealthy, returned the substance if not the form of Miss Dolittle's famous answer.

Bournemouth, Southport, Ilkley, Harrogate, and their counterparts were the Baths and Cheltenhams of this new age. North Oxford, Sefton Park and Edgbaston were its Bloomsburys. But whereas the eighteenth century had expressed its citizenship in continuous street square and crescent, these new places proclaimed Romance and Individualism in large separate villas all well set back from curving park-like roads among sheltering trees, wild rockeries and geranium-dotted carpet beds.

All these changes, these moralisings, these delights, were only, of course, for the powerful. Such subtleties were not for members of the insensate mob. These human ciphers had nothing to do with Romance or the expression of individuality, for they had neither. They were merely the main part of the machine that turned out the profits. And all that was necessary for them, when they were not in use, was to be packed into the various compartments of the long brick box that the Street had now become. So while it was being destroyed for the wealthy, ignorance of its origins and indifference to its essential nature were causing the Street to be debased to that final limit of degradation which led to a universal revulsion against it, and so to its ultimate destruction.

Before this general revulsion set in, however, the

worker had already, in two special instances, been given his release. In 1879 at Bournville, and in 1888 at Port Sunlight, two socially-conscious industrialists had established for their employees places as romantic as Bournemouth or North Oxford; places where little cottages, in imitation of the vernacular cottages of the countryside, faced on to village greens; where after factory hours a somewhat slender semblance to rural life might be led digging in idyllic gardens under the benevolent eye of a philanthropic proprietor. Here were glimpses even for the dwellers in byelaw streets of an alternative to those grim places that had come to seem inevitable to them. Here especially were shining examples to social reformers of what might yet be done, not merely for the rich or even for the comfortable, but for the drab millions of the proletariat itself.

Thus, then, had the way been prepared for the revolt against the Victorian Camp. Thus by the end of the century had the times become propitious for the acceptance of whatever ideal might offer the furthest possible escape from the beastliness of the various Batleys and Bootles, the various Mansfields and Middlesbroughs which now represented the English conception of the town.

The finest possible ideal, from this point of view, was that which Ebenezer Howard now set out in his book *To-morrow* (1898). It was no very new Utopia. Some of its features had already been outlined by James Silk Buckingham for that 'Victoria' which had failed to achieve reality fifty years earlier; and for the rest they were founded on the romantic philosophy which had already for so long been undermining the old urban tradition and which had been given material form in Bournemouth and Port Sunlight. But though these instruments of destruction were by no means new, they were wielded by Howard with a new vigour, their thrust was given a new twist that made an end at last not only

84

Port Sunlight: a group of cottages. From a drawing by
T. Raffles Davison, 1916.

of the Victorian conception of the town but of every
conception of it which had prevailed since man came
out of barbarism.

For Howard was not content with desiring to bring
into the town the expression of the new romantic æsthetic. He preached the old town's complete destruction.
Even as late as 1848 it had still been possible for a
reformer like Buckingham to accept the traditional idea
of the town, to believe fervently in its capacity for
beauty, in its progressive influence, in its worthiness to
be the habitation of civilised man. That was possible no
longer. Now to the romantic mind the town was essentially hateful, incapable of beauty, an evil thing to be
destroyed. And the Georgian town being swamped and
ignored, what better support could be desired for this
contention than the sprawling camps of Tyneside, Clyde-
side, the Potteries, or even the byelaw streets of a
hundred southern towns still comparatively immune
from industrial influence?

F

But if the town was evil, what was the alternative to it? There was, of course, the countryside; that English countryside whose green undulations lapped right up against the filthy frontiers of the towns to make them look the more shameful. There surely, in those clean paradisial expanses, was beauty and peace that all men should enjoy. "Back to the Land" was already an old cry, and Howard raised it again. Yet even here there was a worm in the bud. Not without result had the prophet been born within the sound of Bow Bells. True Cockney, he found the country lovely but intolerably lonely. Here then was his dilemma. The town, though it once had been "the symbol of broad expanding sympathies, of science, art, culture, religion", is hideous and evil. "And the country . . . . the symbol of God's love and care for men . . . . is very dull for lack of society and very sparing of her gifts for lack of Capital." Which of these two age-old antitheses should provide man with his perfect habitation? Which, indeed, when both were faulty? Yet why either? There was, for the romantic mind, a very simple way out of a difficulty like this. "The fullness of joy and wisdom has not yet revealed itself to man. Nor can it ever, so long as this unholy, unnatural separation of Society and Nature endures. Town and Country *must be married*, and out of their joyous union will spring a new hope, a new life, a new civilization"; a marriage which "may be illustrated by a diagram of the *Three Magnets* in which the chief advantages of the Town and of the Country are set forth with their corresponding drawbacks, while the advantages of Town-Country are seen to be free from the disadvantages of either."

It was on pseudo-philosophical foundations like this that the New Jerusalems were builded. The acceptance of such romanticism may perhaps be regarded as an indication of the desperate condition to which social reformers had been reduced; but, be that as it may, the

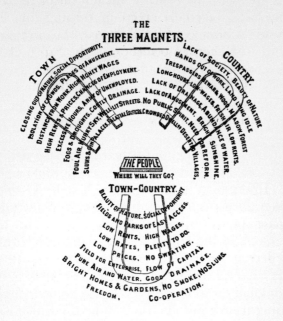

Ebenezer Howard's Magnets, from Tomorrow:
A Peaceful Path to Real Reform: 1898.

acceptance was there, and it was enthusiastic and
sincere. Within a year or two of Howard's publication
of *To-morrow*, there had been promoted, largely because
of his own determination and initiative, a company to
translate Town-Country into actual fact; the First
Garden City was springing up among the Hertfordshire
meadows at Letchworth; a Garden Suburb was building
at Hampstead; and Garden Villages were rising in
different parts of the country at the bidding of various
conscience-stricken industrialists.

In all these places the simple purity of the initial
Town-Country form was much modified by practical
considerations. In one place, indeed, in Hampstead
Garden Suburb, these practical modifications went so

87

far that somehow or other a suggestion of the genuine town itself managed to creep in through one or two small-scale groupings which followed, though hesitantly, the eighteenth-century tradition of the Street. But such lapses were rare. Above all a country flavour must be achieved. In Town-Country the country must prevail. In Garden-City (which was, of course, the same thing) the emphasis must all be on the garden. So all the houses were now to be country cottages set singly or in pairs along curving countrified roads diversified with hedges, trees, and shrubs, herbaceous borders and green swards. Informality and romance was the key-note. In fact when all was said and done Town-Country arrived as but a popular edition of Bournemouth and the rest of the resorts of the Victorian upper-middle classes.

It reflected, indeed, precisely the same attitude of mind as those places had reflected. The artisan and the clerk who had for so long suffered repression in Victorian streets might now indulge their individualistic yearnings no less than their superiors. This in truth was one of the main attractions of Town-Country. From the very beginning Howard had laid down the individualistic nature of his Utopia. In it there was to be no physical reflection of the co-operative basis of community life. That "the fullest measure of individual taste and preference is encouraged" he had offered as a principal reason for its acceptance. In the building of Letchworth the declared aim was that "each house will stand in its own garden", while an instruction to participants stated that "ample frontage will be provided and it is hoped that builders will not think of erecting those common unsatisfactory rows of narrow houses". Now, then, the Street is dead at last. And so that there may be no mistake about it the very word is forbidden in Town-Country even for the purpose of address.

Town-Country might in actual practice seem to fall short of that great ideal which was to provide "a new hope, a new life, a new civilization". But in spite of this, or perhaps because of it, it did not for long remain, as so many Utopias have remained, the merely private panacea of a small band of enthusiastic dreamers. Before the persuasive eloquence of its advocates even the natural conservatism of Parliament itself gave way, and in the course of a few years not only had conformation to Town-Country ideals been made compulsory in the thousands of housing schemes which Government itself was forced by circumstances to undertake, but, so far had enthusiasm advanced, it was enforced (under what was ironically enough called a Town Planning Act) upon private persons building for private purposes. Here was a remarkable situation. Forced at last by the miseries of the Victorian town into active intervention, the Government, for the first time in the history of England, was now taking a hand in the planning of towns. And the principles which it was enforcing towards that end had originally been advocated for nothing short of the town's destruction. Now indeed Howard's hopes had reached a remarkable fulfilment. He had cried "Back to the Land" and had offered Town-Country as the instrument for producing that return. And now every dock worker in Liverpool, every cotton operative in Bolton, every clerk, every shopkeeper, every artisan in all the big and little towns in the kingdom must henceforward, according to law and whether they liked it or not, live under conditions intended for part-time peasants.

All this activity arose simply and directly out of the sincere and only too natural desire of social reformers to create a better place than the Victorian town for twentieth-century Englishmen. It was an artificially-created activity prompted largely by æsthetic ideals. But though the times were propitious for its success, not even Howard himself could have seen quite how propitious. Even before the foundation stone of Letchworth had been laid there had come about changes through which Town-Country would probably have materialised of its own accord.

The first, and perhaps the chief, and certainly most easily measurable of these changes was a series of mechanical inventions which threw down most of the historical barriers between town and country. Before the invention of the steam locomotive those barriers had been complete. The railways and later a few tramways had made sufficient breaches in them for the overflow of the manufacturing towns to spill out in short thin ribbons or gather into new groups within the fixed and narrow limits of their influence. But now the motor car and the motor bus shattered the ancient barriers completely. They ran out from the towns into the countryside along all the strands of an intricate thickly-woven network of roads, and with them they carried ten million townsmen sick of their byelaw streets, wearied of their sordid towns; carried them out and set them down on their new doorsteps, five, ten, fifteen miles away from town.

Another invention, the radio, afforded these people in their new places many of the social pleasures which only the town had hitherto provided. And while the townsman was thus brought into the countryside, the countryman himself, either indirectly by radio, or directly by bus, was brought far closer within the sphere of urban influence than ever he had been before.

And still another mechanical development assisted in the breakdown of the old barriers. It had been the location of raw materials (in the absence of a really adaptable form of transport), and of power, that had created the industrial town. Now not only was the first of these determining factors changed by the coming of motor transport, but the second also was modified by the development of widespread electricity transmission which made available even in the parish of Cowclap

90

Green a source of power as plentiful and as dependable as that in the city of Coketown.

These changes automatically brought with them changes in building practice. And these (so deep had the hatred of the town become) operated in a precisely similar manner to the changes artificially brought about by Town-Country ideals. It was not only that the population squandered out loosely into the countryside. The already discredited idea of the Street was still further discredited in the necessity for the accommodation of innumerable cars in their own little houses alongside the houses of their owners. And so to the social and æsthetic appeal of Town-Country there was now added the justification of practical advantage.

But added to all these mechanical changes and their results was a sociological change of profound importance. The cry of "Votes for Women" has left its effect on the English town almost as markedly as has that of "Back to the Land". This is not the place to try to analyse the influence of the New Woman (as she was then called) on the architectural standards of to-day, though it is more than probable that upon that influence a good deal of the responsibility for the sham antique and the meretriciously decorative in recent building must lie. But, be that as it may, this at least may be regarded as certain— the Emancipated Woman (who claims the home as her special sphere and demands the right to choose it) has had more than a small share in influencing the form in which Motorville, the mechanically-determined counterpart of Town-Country, has been built. Woman is by nature far more individualistic than man: she has a sense of property and a desire to display it (which the Building Society movement has assisted her to indulge) that is far more highly developed than his: she is at once more conservative and more open to the appeal of small novelty: in æsthetic matters she has few of the makings of a citizen. All these qualities are reflected in a thousand

91

Motorvilles; and it may indeed be said that if the eighteenth-century town glorified man, the Citizen, these places were built for woman, the Individualist supreme.

Yet in spite of the powerful nature of all these changes, they could not have been given their recent widespread expression in the countryside had not still another change come about to place almost the whole landscape at their disposal. In the period between the wars the decline of agriculture and the breaking-up of the old large estates among a multiplicity of small owners weakened almost to nothing the resistance of the countryside against the various disruptive agencies that attacked it. Since these agencies were organised on a national scale, the small units of parish and farm were powerless to withstand their invasion. They were also almost entirely urban or suburban in their outlook. So for the first time in history the English countryside lay entirely at the mercy of the towns.

Here, then, by these various means, by the Victorian debasement of the town, by new mechanical advancements, by social changes and changing sociological ideals, but most of all by the change of mental attitude engendered by the Romantic Revival, we arrived at the destruction of the ideals of the traditional town. In less than two decades ten million people were housed and rehoused by the feverish efforts of authority and private initiative in the greatest period of intensive building the world has ever known. For these people and by them a new form was created. Town and Country were more than married, they were mingled. Everywhere around us to-day we see the fruits of this mingling. Are they, we may justifiably ask, the fine fruits that Howard promised—"a new life, a new hope, a new civilization"? Does Town-Country display, as was prophesied, all the splendid and none of the unpleasant characteristics of the parents it has been begotten on? Or does it rather bring to mind that story reported of the famous beauty, who, approaching an equally famous intellectual male with the request that he should become the father of a eugenic child by her, a child which with her beauty and his brains would be the paragon of the world, was reminded that, alas, the child was as likely to have her brains and his beauty, in which case it would turn out to be a monster of unsightly idiocy?

Town-Country has indeed proved to be the reverse of Howard's hopes. It has also on one major point developed into the reverse of his intentions. For whereas it now sprawls disastrously, the imagined Town-Country was to be in lumps of a strictly limited size organised on that theory of satellite town development which Howard had adopted from James Silk Buckingham. It is regrettable that this borrowed and creative idea should have been ignored, and only Howard's romantic ones should have been accepted. But such would seem to be the way with good and bad ideas in a muddled world. So over a period of about forty years Town-Country developed into something at which Howard himself would have stood aghast. While it has few of the 'advantages' of either the town or the country, it has most of their 'disadvantages'. It is in fact nothing but a universal suburbia, an æsthetic void, a social wilderness. Some measure of its qualities is suggested in the number of societies it has produced for the preservation of the countryside. And if it has not yet produced a society for the preservation of the town, that is merely an indication of how deep was the blow struck by the nineteenth century at the very root of the town conception.

So universal suburbia sprawls drearily about. Loosely (though sincerely) it was conceived: loosely and ever still more loosely it developed down the 1920's and the 1930's. At bottom a social and an aesthetic ideal it displayed ever more deeply as it grew the fundamental falsities of its inspiration. The 'Town' part of it is but a straggling disorder of unrelated buildings and unrelated

93

vacuities. The 'Country' part is a cockney sham where a privet hedge and a root of Michaelmas daisies pitifully symbolise the now all too absent beauties of the country-side. With its formula of one-plus-one-plus-one *ad infinitum* it has resulted in the covering of the greatest possible space with the least positive aesthetic result. Vague, wasteful, formless, incoherent, it has slobbered over the counties. Before its advance the traditional beauties alike of the town and of the country have fallen away and have been succeeded by a dull characterless neutrality. Striving everywhere to escape from the towns to the countryside its inhabitants have thwarted themselves and each other, pushing the object of their desire ever further beyond their reach. London has so stretched out to embrace the country that the country is now twenty miles further from London.

And the dwellers in the suburbs are twenty miles further from town. And consequently they may be twenty miles further from their work—in which Town-Country displays its failure from a sociological as well as from an æsthetic point of view. For, in spite of the operation of the so-called Town Planning Acts of the 1920's and 1930's, the growth of Town-Country was even more a matter of blind chance than was the growth of the Victorian town. Then the limited nature of the transport facilities bound factories as well as houses within a limited circuit. Now, both being unbound and unorganised, these essentially inter-related necessities of modern living were set up separately where nothing but chance or a merely personal whim dictated. Inevitably ease of transport brought increase of transport. Criss-cross from one part to another, but most of all backwards and forwards upon the town centre, the ever-increasing traffic gets more and more congested, and time and money and energy are drained away in a colossal folly of unproductive movement till it has become a curious commentary on unorganised Town-Country that the inhabitants of it must not only spend considerable portions of their lives travelling to and from this "new life, new hope, new civilization", but must often deny themselves some of the necessities of existence to be able to do so.

The plain fact is that in Town-Country there is no new hope—nor any hope at all. For what hope in the modern world can spring from a chaos of individualism? And that is precisely what Town-Country was, and is. Semi-detached houses in a sham-rural street in a wilderness of semi-detached houses in sham-rural streets are indeed something more than a chaos of romantic individualism in themselves: they were, and are to-day, the physical expression of the prime social evil of their time. Everywhere, in the decades when they were built, individualism was supreme: and the Street and the Town, those two creations in which the quality of man's mass association had hitherto been so clearly symbolised, unmistakably illustrated it—by their very absence.

It was individualism with a difference, of course. Not the crude Victorian individualism of the successful few which involved the ruthless repression of the many. It was, in truth, the extremity of reaction from that: a romantic universal individualism in which every man gloried, and was encouraged to glory, in his self-sufficiency and separateness.

So there are no citizens in Town-Country. There are only inhabitants of it. There is no community. There is only a collection of separate units. The Individual, not the Citizen, is glorified there. Blind, uncontrolled, drugged with romanticism, drunk with a false independence, universal suburbia has sprawled wastefully on. Sprawled whither? Towards a new beauty and a new hope, or merely towards a dull dead-level of neutrality, a new and more tangled chaos?

Well, we already have more than enough Town-Country to judge from.

95

And what of those parts of the countryside that were not absorbed into suburbia? What has happened during these forty years, to that humanised landscape which a few generations of Englishmen nearly two centuries ago created with loving and energetic enterprise?

Here in contrast to the all too feverish activity in suburbia the story has been one of inaction and neglect, and our sins only the more pitiful ones of omission. The attitude engendered by the Romantic Revival here at last had its results. When "mountains are the beginning and the end of all natural scenery", when only places that are untouched by human activity arouse a deep emotional response, man soon arrives at a stage when the humanised scene leaves him indifferent, and any activity there other than economic activity seems at best to be but wasted effort. And that, almost, was what it came to during these recent decades. The result of it would have been melancholy enough had the landscape here been that universal landscape where man's effort has only rarely been directed towards æsthetic ends. But the English countryside being what it is, neglect was all the more melancholy since it fell upon what had once been the object of such devotion and high endeavour.

For the man-directed landscape must be man-maintained. The trees and hedges that compose it suffer a natural decay: they need to be replaced as they die. And furthermore it is in this century that the incidence of decay must fall on these elements of England's beauty. The modern rural scene was begun two hundred years ago. It reached its maturity at the middle and end of last century. Now and within the next few decades, unless effort is made to maintain it, it must fall to ruin as the country which man made and which God has unmade.

But no effort has been made during this century towards this maintenance. Besides the toll which natural decay has taken, the wholesale felling of timber that necessarily went on during the two great wars and the destruction that has thoughtlessly occurred in road widening and similar works all down the century has done much to change for the worse the appearance of the country scene even within the memory of the comparatively young. Already many districts have been denuded of much timber. And scarcely a hand has been lifted to repair the damage that has been wrought, hardly a sapling has been planted to replace the thousands of "splendidly broad-shouldered, ancient, generous, free, venerable vast trees" that have gone. It is true that extensive afforestation has been undertaken by the Government; but this, in its concentration on conifers instead of hardwoods, has done as much to destroy the traditional scene as the fellings themselves; and in any case, even if hardwoods had been used, this practice of large-scale forestry would not have maintained a scene which depends for its effect on single-standing or small-grouped trees and copses, and not at all upon extensive woodlands. It is also true that some planting was undertaken in the 1930's along the new roads that were built; but this again was almost always undertaken, through ignorance or indifference, in precisely that alien manner of planting miles of avenues which the English landscapists discarded two hundred years ago. So even where there has been some consciousness of the evil days upon which the landscape has fallen, it has been only the more pitiful when the actions of the conscious few have shown how far they were removed from any understanding of the spirit that created our inheritance.

A similar fate to that of the trees has befallen the hedgerows. Through age and neglect these great though modest instruments of England's beauty have also fallen into decay. During these forty years hundreds of miles of old hedgerows have disappeared from the scene, and have been replaced, if at all, by mechanical fencing

97

which presented the aspect of dilapidation almost from the day it was first put up. It is safe to say that hardly a single hawthorn plant has been set in the hedges of the countryside (except on a few new roads) throughout the whole course of this century.

The same tale could be told of almost all the various features of the rural landscape. During the agricultural depression of the 1930's, especially, barns and byres fell into dilapidation and were patched and held together, if at all, with any old piece of material, however incongruous, that came first to hand. Many of the older cottages and farmhouses had become ruinous and insanitary: the new were built with all the shoddiness and vulgarity of the meanest suburbs. So were the village extensions—for these in any case were mostly made for retired and week-ending townsmen. The land itself deteriorated. Even the quality of the grassland declined to an alarming degree. Substantial areas of once valuable and productive land went back to bracken and gorse and rank marsh—to say nothing of the 70,000 acres which went every year for buildings and various kinds of "public works". The English countryside of the 1930's, to those who could read its meaning, was a disturbing and melancholy landscape.

And if this was the position of the countryside, what happened to the old town? While the "new hope, new life, new civilization" of suburbia was pursued down the highways and byways, what happened to that old symbol of despair, the Victorian camp?

Alas! that in cities, more than elsewhere, the evil men do should live after them! Little enough happened to the camp. Despite all the activity in new building, the old core remained, unaltered save by age, its earlier parts almost as foul as ever they were, as squalid, as congested; its later parts as grim, as sanitary and as dull: all darkened now by the years of smoke that have passed over them, made more melancholy by the dead lives that have been dragged out in their vast hopelessness. The camp is very permanent. The Sheffields, the Rotherhams, the Middlesbroughs, the Batleys, the Coketowns, the Byelawtowns live on almost unchanged.

This then is what we had come to in that epoch which ended in 1939. The old town, a repellent mass of dreary rows of mean houses surrounding, sometimes, an old core where the light of a more gracious age still lingered, but encompassing, for the most part, a commercial centre where the meanness was corrupted by a vulgarity that made it even more shameful. The countryside, that once was at its doors, now pushed away behind miles of vague and disorderly suburbs; and everywhere disorder, waste, and a bitter meanness of spirit. Where once beauty was a quality that quickened men to joy, where once the glory of the town was the pride and the sacrifice of its citizens, now nothing mattered save the day's profit, a night's pleasure, and then—escape for those who could. The Street had gone, and with it the whole conception of the town that it symbolised. The story had run almost to full circle. And truly indeed might that tortured prophet D. H. Lawrence now cry: "As the makers of towns the English are more ignominious than rabbits."

CHAPTER SIX

TO-MORROW

IT HAS BEEN A MELANCHOLY STORY, this that we have traced of the English scene's fall from its high attainment of the eighteenth century to its recent degradation. It would be a bitter story too, if that were the end of it.

Until recently it seemed that it might indeed be the end of it. There was not only the enormous actuality of suburbs that had been spilt far and wide; there was also, for those who knew of it, that forecast, contemporaneous with Ebenezer Howard's Utopia, in which H. G. Wells, so often wise before the event, had anticipated those suburbs with extraordinary accuracy, and in which he had prophesied, for no very distant date, the final dissolution of the town in a 'countryside' sprouting Tudor cottages as frequently as trees. "The same lines of reasoning", Wells had written in his *Anticipations* (1900),

that leads to the expectation that the city will diffuse itself until it has taken up considerable areas and many of the characteristics, the greenness, the fresh air of what is now country, leads us to suppose also that the country will take to itself many of the qualities of the city. The old antithesis will indeed cease, the boundary lines will altogether disappear: it will become indeed merely a question of more or less population.

Was this already half-realised anticipation in truth to come fully to pass? Was it, after all, possible that the recent degradation was but the prelude to final destruction? Was the town, that instrument of so much of our past development, to disappear; to be discarded like a thing that has served its purpose and is now required no longer: to be superseded, as some mechanism grown inefficient through constant misuse is superseded, by a glittering new invention retailed on easy terms and with rosy promises? Was the countryside, that most noble of all the English works of art, that supreme achievement of our civilization, also to be destroyed and disappear? Was it now, in short, to be a universal cry of "The Town is dead: the Country is dead: long live Town-Country"? These were questions which a few troubled people were asking in the 1930's.

They were not merely rhetorical questions. They had the accent of urgency in them. And they still have. Upon the answers to them the whole character of the civilization of the future may turn. And without any doubt they are questions which are vital to our consideration here, for before we can attempt to discuss the possible future of the town and the countryside it is clearly necessary to consider whether they have any future to discuss.

In one particular direction at any rate the town's and indeed the countryside's future is more than a little uncertain unless men quickly achieve a change of heart. If ever war occurs again among the technically advanced nations of the world, then cities and whole regions will be reduced to uninhabitable ruin, and the whole social and economic system will be so shaken that the recovery from the cataclysm, if recovery there be, will in every likelihood be along a road which will lead to an entirely different mode of life. But that, however overwhelming and tragic its import, is a matter which is outside our consideration here. What *is* within our consideration is whether man has now reached a stage in his development when he is able to dispense with the old medium, the town, which has brought him so far along the road to civilization, and whether he is capable to-day of creating a new medium which **may** serve him better.

If there is such a new medium, and if it is attainable under modern conditions of life, then it should be seized upon with delight and with few regrets for the town which it would displace; for the town is of no value except in so far as it serves and satisfies the purposes of man. But while it is possible that such a medium may be attained in the distant future, it is difficult to believe that it is available now. Certainly the form with which we unconsciously experimented in the 1930's can by no means be regarded as satisfactory. It is probable indeed that Town-Country, and the whole romantic attitude from which it springs, is not only incapable of advancing the development of human happiness but must actually impede it. But in any case the very fact that the Town-Country medium has in practice degenerated to what it is to-day is a clear answer to the question of whether or not man has yet developed so far that it is possible for him to desert the town.

It is true, as we have already seen, that the recent inventions which have extended the facilities for communication, whether they be the improved means of transport extending physical communication or the radio and television extending social intercourse, have in many ways weakened the domination of the town. But at least as important as that is the fact that they have enormously widened the sphere of its attraction by bringing within its disturbing influence even the remotest hamlets and cottages of the wide countryside. Thus at a time when the so-called 'flight from the town' was regarded as crucial and self-evident, the far older 'flight from the countryside' continued as ever it had done. So much so that, in 1939, more than 80 per cent. of the total population of England and Wales lived in urban and suburban areas; and around one centre alone, on the banks of the Thames, there was and is now gathered something like one-fifth of the population of the entire country. Which would seem to be an indication that, however strong may be their romantic yearnings for the countryside, the English people cannot easily steel themselves against the attractions which the town alone continues to provide.

But even if they would willingly desert the town is it, under our present civilization, economically possible for them to do so? Theoretically the new mobility of transport and the widespread distribution of power have freed mechanised industry and its workers from many of the fetters which during the period of the Industrial Revolution bound its various units together in certain fixed geographical centres. Yet other and more powerful bonds remain; and to-day our economic life is founded, even more than it was fifty or a hundred years ago, on the group-association of large masses of people in particular places. What our mechanical advancement has done is to free industry geographically, but not economically or socially; a fact again which is illustrated by the attractions of London, the industrial drift to whose outskirts has been one of the most notable features of the present century.

Thus, then, we may say that, under our present civilization, no matter how far mechanical invention may proceed, man's social instincts and the basic needs of the industrial system will almost inevitably maintain the mass-grouping of the majority of people in some form or other of urban association. As a nation we are irrevocably committed to an urban way of life. And that being so, it surely behoves us to see that the form of our urban association, and the physical mould in which it operates, are given an organisation, a shape, and an expression which will afford in the fullest possible degree the profit and pleasure which is the town's essential purpose.

That such a state of affairs is desirable there can be no doubt. But to achieve it we shall have to effect a considerable change in ourselves. For the town is far more than a material and economic fact. It is also an atmosphere, an attitude of mind. And that is precisely where the English town has gone wrong since the early decades of the nineteenth century. It has been regarded merely as an economic necessity: its social idea has been lost, forgotten, ignored. Because of this, the complementary reaction of debasement has destroyed the loyalties that the town should inspire. And this in time has bred the longing to escape. All the poets, philosophers, prophets, and architects whose guidance might have counteracted the materialism of the times, and so have rehabitated the town after its initial debasement, have preached nothing but romantic escape from the inevitable to the impossible. Every one of the manifestations of the Romantic Agony from Pugin's *Contrasts* to Howard's *Garden Cities* was an incitement to it. For a hundred years we have behaved like film-struck servant girls blinded to the filth accumulating around us by romantic dreams of worlds as yet and ever likely to be unrealised. More than anything else it has been this pitiful attitude of escape which has brought the English town from its beauty and hopefulness of a hundred and fifty years ago to its shapeless and shameful meanness of to-day.

The town being inevitable for us, we shall have once and for all to be done with escapism and with the romanticism which breeds it. Already indeed there is clearly discernible a revulsion not only against the still surviving desolation of the Victorian camp, but also against the ideals of escapism which helped to create it and then led us into the suburban wilderness. Even the legislation of the day is beginning to reflect this. The revulsion, it is true, is still manifested chiefly in concern for the countryside. But then for more than a century the average Englishman has never known the beauty, the poetry, nor even the mere convenience of which the true town is capable. When once again he is shown by actual example what the true town may be in contrast to the camp and the suburb to which he has become habituated; when once again the tradition which gave at least parts of the English towns a native seemliness no less triumphant than the beauty of the countryside is broadened and adapted to meet the needs of these later times; then at last he will be as concerned for the creation of beauty in the town as he is now concerned for the preservation of the remaining beauty of the countryside.

And that is where the hope for the future lies. For we must do more than get rid of escapism. The mere acceptance of the inevitable, the making the best of a bad job, will not lead us out of confusion. Since towns are inevitable we should surely build good towns. How can we build good towns if we continue to despise the town?

The good town must exist as an idea before it can be created as a fact. The first need for building good towns is a realisation not only of the inevitability of the town but of its actual desirability as an ideal in itself; a medium through which not only may the material comforts of life be obtained, but a good life be lived; an instrument which is capable not only of the production of the good life but of a triumphant and inspiring beauty of its own. In a word, we can only build the good town when we believe again, as the eighteenth-century builders believed, in its possibility.

The good town is the place in which a good life may be lived. That indeed is the great point. A place to *live* in. For a hundred years the town has been regarded simply as a place to work in—which is why it is what it is. We shall need to destroy that base conception. A place for living is what we must strive to create if ever we are to rehabilitate the town. And not merely a place to live in but a place in which the social as well as the individual life may be lived; a place where men may live and work, not as separate units each with an exclusively individual aim and end, but as members of a body dwelling together in co-operative association; a place which will house a community; which will both serve and stimulate communal purpose, but which will, at the same time, provide for and facilitate the achievement of personal happiness among its individual inhabitants. A place, that is, built for man, the Citizen.

If this is what the town of the future is to be, how are we to set about its attainment? Through what formulae, by what plan, are we to raise this shining edifice? For clearly, above all, some plan, some predetermined line of action, is necessary for an undertaking of this nature. If the past has taught us anything at all, it has at least taught us that.

Since the prime social idea behind the town is the satisfaction of the needs of the individual within the framework of the community, the question of the attainment of the good town will probably resolve itself into the recognition of the existence of various social units requiring and making possible certain communal advantages, and the building upon those units of a sound social structure. In the past the standard social unit was the family. That unit was for long so self-contained that its existence was a prime obstacle to communal development; and indeed the history of the town is to some extent the history of the gradual breakdown, or at least the restriction, of its domination. Now, through various causes, some economic, some social, and some biological, the family is no longer the exclusive and dominating power that it was, and other units within the modern community which are far larger than that must be recognised and fostered. What exactly they will be, we are hardly yet in a position to say. The next smallest unit to the family may possibly prove to be the smallest group of families that is necessary to require and maintain an elementary social institution such as a crèche, or a nursery school. Upon this smallest communal unit other units may be built in a similar way until the whole town and the region have been loosely organised for the fulfilment of all their social purposes. Thus it may be possible to say that a minimum of such and such a number of 'crèche units' is necessary to support (and therefore create) a 'health centre unit', or a 'primary school unit'; then so many of these to the 'secondary school unit'; and so on through all the social services of the town and the region. Something of this sort has indeed already been established in recent years in that theory of 'neighbourhood planning' which has become one of the prime bases of town planning not only in England but in other parts of the world as well.

Similarly the future system of local government, in the larger towns at any rate, may possibly be based on and expand through this progression of social units, the government of the town being organised so that the individual units may be represented in the administration of the groups, the groups in that of the districts, the districts in that of the town, and so on. By this means, by permitting the small units to have some direct part in the management of affairs affecting them, all the members of a community would have their member-ship made far more apparent than it is to-day, and the community sense would be fostered and citizenship made a far more genuine thing than ever it has been before. Upon this fostering of the community sense, indeed, far more than the success of the town depends. It is not without its importance in the survival of democracy itself.

But even though such arrangements as these may help to bring about in our future towns a satisfaction and a sense of fulfilment which has been absent for a hundred years, there is a further consideration which is no less important in achieving the good town which has been adumbrated. The modern attitude of escape from the town, even if it is only to a suburb, has arisen in part

at least from the fact that many of our towns have been almost completely cut off from contact with the countryside. This divorce men cannot healthily endure. Sheer physical urbanity gives of its most stimulating delights, both visually and socially, only when it is easily escapable. The great and inescapable city becomes overbearingly oppressive—and so in a different, a more deadening, more tantalising way does the great and still-imprisoning suburbia through which we have attempted to escape from it. The clear alternative to both these evils is the reasonably-sized sheerly-urban town, with a beginning, a middle, and an end—the town which, while offering the benefits and pleasures traditionally associated with urban conditions, will still have within approachable distance of any part of it the so different yet complementary pleasures of the countryside. The good town is still, even in these days of swift mechanical transport, that which is built on the ancient precept that a man can walk out of it on his own legs. It should therefore be as compact as possible, while at the same time maintaining the proper requirements of light and air and having enough open places to walk in and play in. Many new demands will tend to make the towns of the future far bigger in physical size than the towns of the past have been—the demand for great areas of playing fields for schools, for example; and even that sub-division of the town into separate neighbourhoods which has just been spoken of. In the interests of the countryside as well as of the town we shall need to guard against this temptation, for in a country as heavily populated as ours we can no longer afford to be as improvident with our land as we have been in the recent past. But even though we aim at compactness, the redevelopment of the old heavily-congested districts which house most of our urban population to-day will mean that, unless we plan to avoid it, our towns must grow bigger. For already
108

over-big cities such further growth would be disastrous. So in the future we will need to build new towns in accordance with that theory of urban growth propounded by James Silk Buckingham a hundred years ago and first put into practice by Ebenezer Howard at Letchworth and Welwyn. Some such towns are already coming into being under government patronage at Stevenage, Harlow, Hemel Hempstead, Crawley and other places. But the first plans for these new towns are still clouded with garden-city suburbanism: and future building in similar places, and in all old towns, will need to be more compact and more truly urban than these first new ventures are at present planned to be.

If these are the lines along which the sociological and physical bases of the town may be organised in the future, what is likely to be its physical form?

In the central parts of the larger towns, at least, there are likely to be striking changes in appearance. These will arise out of the necessity of avoiding to-day's traffic congestion and out of the need to give the interiors of buildings far better light and air than they now have. The permissible height bulk and use of buildings will have to be related to the pattern and widths of the streets adjoining them: and the well-like interior courts that characterise central-city buildings to-day will need to be opened out. Here the continuous façade of the Street as it has hitherto been known will give place to a more broken and more open form in which adjoining buildings will have recessed and even separated tower-like upper storeys. Here also there will be elevated or sunken roadways carrying fast traffic clear of building frontages. These changed scenes may bring a new and striking beauty or a still more frantic disorder into the great city, according to how far, and with what imagination and skill, their planners have been able to design and control them—an operation in planning, this, beside which the renaissance form of civic design will seem but the innocent play of an uncomplicated age.

These changes will be far less spectacular than those which have been imagined in many fantastic forecasts of the shape of things to come. The aerial roads,

Pitched between Heaven and Charing Cross,

the topless towers and all the rest of the rather nightmarish properties of Corbusierean fantasy may perhaps materialise some day. But they are some time distant yet, even for the great metropolitan cities: and we can safely leave them outside our anticipations for the ordinary town of to-morrow, or even of the day after.

In England that town will retain, it is to be hoped, something of its traditional form and appearance in its broadest aspects. Not, of course, in its details: for while the characteristic examples of traditional building that still remain in most old towns should certainly be preserved and maintained in the future, it would be as futile as it would be mean-spirited to imitate the details of that building in our new work. It is the characteristic quality rather than the detailed forms of those towns that we shall need to strive after,—that quality of ordered domesticity and intimacy in architectural effects which is the peculiarly English contribution to the art of town building. Yet if we recapture something of the old attitude we are likely also to approximate to something of the architectural form in which that attitude was expressed. Thus, in spite of the particular demands and influences which may create different effects in the central parts of large cities, we may properly expect, in most parts of most towns, a return to that building in terrace formation which is the natural architectural expression of citizenship as well as the architectural form which similar building-units in close association naturally develop.

But in returning to the terrace and to the use of plan-shapes such as the square, and possibly (though in a freer form) the crescent, we should no more adopt the pure renaissance theories of civic design than our ancestors did. Those theories, and the whole practice of monumental design which was based upon them, are still the established mode for planning towns in many other countries. They have never suited the English temperament. The pure renaissance town was a monument. Its great planned effects were static. They gave an immediate, perhaps a breath-taking sensation: and then had no more to give. In the fully planned renaissance town everything was displayed once and for all: there were no intimate qualities; no secrets: there was nothing to learn, and nothing, by learning, to love. It was a town to look at, to visit, rather than a town to live in. Its one great quality was that it had order. The mediaeval town, on the other hand, was wildly disordered. But in contrast to the renaissance town its effects were full of movement, of variety, of surprise, of changing interest. This was a living town, and a town to look at while one lived in it. This is the kind of town we should have in the future.

To recreate something like the true mediæval town now would, of course, be even more difficult than to recreate the renaissance town. And it would be as futile. Imitation of either would be meaningless. But we can learn from the past without imitating it: and our towns of the future can have the best physical qualities of both the mediæval and the renaissance town if we chose to use and adapt their forms to our new purposes.

The English genius has always lain in the production of harmony in variety. That has characterised our political and social life as well as our architectural forms throughout the long course of our history. And while in the last hundred years the physical expression of the native genius has been so vitiated that there was neither harmony nor variety in our town building, the genius is within us still if we care to give it again its freedom of expression.

Harmony in variety: variety in harmony: form without formality: order without repression or regimentation—all this we can express in our towns of to-morrow. And in expressing it we shall be but renewing the English tradition. From our individual expression of renaissance building we can adapt the characteristic terrace to our newer, freer, less formal planning. From the mediaeval town we can adapt the plan-forms which made the town an unfolding succession of changing scenes. And in so doing we will give a renewed and a modern expression to the tradition of the town as an intimate domestic place for living in as free citizens. Not a camp nor a monument, but simply a home. Thus once again we can, if we will, build the town as " the school of the social arts, the nursery of social enterprise, the witness to the beauty and order and freedom that men can bring into their lives". And in our planning of that town we shall do well to keep in mind these words of W. R. Lethaby: "To forget the past would be as foolish as to ignore the future. Behind is custom, as in front is adventure. We have to awaken the civic ideal and to aim first at the obvious commonplace of cleanliness, order and efficiency. Much has to be done: it is a time of beginning as well as of making an end."

§

If for the town it is a time of beginning as well as of making an end, then surely it should be a time of renewal for the countryside also.

It is no mere empty phrase to say that the fate of the countryside depends on the future of the town. Since the ravage of suburbia resulted from the building of uninhabitable towns, so its future avoidance, and the countryside's salvation, lies largely in the town's being once more made a place fit to live in. When that has been achieved, when the town has been brought back to self-respect, we may expect an end of Town-Country. From that time will date the renewal of the countryside. And perhaps the pride of creating the new town may bring, as it brought under the Renaissance, a new understanding to our activities in the landscape also.

But the relationship between these two parts of the scene has changed. The realisation of that is perhaps the first necessity for bringing about the countryside's regeneration. The old balance between town and country has gone and will never return. The town will always be dominant now, and a new form of interplay between the two must be organised.

What will that new form of interplay be? For the answer to that question we must look again at to-day's suburbia. If we are to have done with escapism then we must not only make pleasant the life and character of the confining town, we must give its willing prisoners the key to the outside world. The fundamental consideration to be observed in the new relationship between town and country will therefore be that the townsman of the future must be given his own stake in the country-side. The times are past when the country was the province only of the countryman. The townsman must now be given his share in that province. If he is not, even the good town of the future will burst its bonds and the floods of surburbia will again be let loose. Above everything the compact sheerly urban town which we hope may come into being depends upon its having free access to the countryside at its doors.

That access will need to be provided in diverse forms. The road system is bound to be extensively changed and improved, and we may expect the great arteries of to-morrow's traffic to bring a new and, if they are properly designed, a not necessarily discordant but rather a majestically confident motif into the landscape.

Within the broad pattern of these highways, the little country lanes may regain something of their old peace and intimacy. On a still more intimate scale the existing field-paths and bridle-ways which are so pleasant a feature of England should be brought, through the introduction of new links, into a complete though loosely defined system; and the banks of many rivers and streams as well as the cliffs and dunes of the sea-coast should be made free. But more than this, there will need to be provided occasional wide expanses where the townsman can indulge in unrestricted movement: so woodland areas, parklands, and hillsides will need to be set aside as regional reserves, and wide stretches of coast and whole mountain districts will need to be made free as national parks.

But in addition to the true townsmen who will live in the new towns, there will be numbers of town-employed people, and particularly people who after a lifetime of working in the town desire to spend their last years in the peace of the country, who will demand, as they demand to-day, the right to live in rural surroundings. That right should not be denied them, provided always that it is the right to *live* in the countryside and not merely to convert it into suburbia. There is clearly room in the wide expanses of the rural scene for a great number of new buildings to be absorbed without serious damage to landscape character—so long as they are properly organized in relation to their settings. And looking round at the dreary unassimilated urban intruders in to-day's countryside, what form of organization, we may ask, will be necessary to bring the newcomer of to-morrow to terms with his landscape as well as with his fellow men?

That form of organization is obviously the village. The invaders who in the 1930's pushed out their long attenuated ribbons of roadside houses unconsciously confessed this even in their denial of it. The invaders of

114

the future may actually achieve what those others set out to seek and so pitifully failed to gain—the best of both worlds in social life and rural beauty. But they will only achieve it, they will only in fact avoid the destruction of both the objects of their desire, in a frank expression, not in a denial, of their communal purpose: and it may properly be expected that in the future the townsman desiring to live in the countryside will be content to make his choice of new living place from the ten thousand villages that are even now open to him.

Though some few new villages will, no doubt, need to be built for the purposes of new or much extended countryside activities (such, for example, as the extensive afforestation of hitherto uncultivated lands which is even now being undertaken by government agencies), the housing of any increased population in the countryside should for the most part be by way of additions to existing villages. But the main building activity in old villages will be the rebuilding of the thousands of outworn cottages and farmhouses, or their adaptation in accordance with the improved standards of accommodation now required. The days are gone when the countryman could be expected to live in conditions far below those of the townsman. So the clearance or improvement of rural slums, however picturesque they may be, will need to be regarded as no less urgent than the clearance of their urban counterparts (though it is to be hoped that this will not be undertaken ruthlessly, for where old country buildings can be satisfactorily adapted it will be better to adapt than to destroy them). Through these activities the hitherto neglected satisfaction of one of the countryman's basic individual needs will be met. But that in itself will not be enough. One of the main causes of the drift from the countryside during this century has been the lack of adequate social provisions in satisfactory schools, meeting places, entertainments, playing fields and the like. These, too, will have to be provided. Since they can flourish only when there is a sufficient number of people to maintain them, it may be that people living in some of the smaller hamlets will need to be rehoused elsewhere.* There are, of course, dangers in this. Planners will need to beware of the unimaginative and inhumane application of rigid theories to matters which deeply affect people's lives and liberties. What may sound logical in theory may be both undesirable and impossible in fact. It may well be argued, for example, as indeed it was seriously argued some years ago by a learned professor of geography, that (in view of modern improvements in communications) the historical pattern of villages situated at intervals of two or three miles apart should now be abandoned in favour of small towns spaced at intervals of ten or twenty miles, whence farm workers, while enjoying town amenities, can travel out to their work in the fields each day by motor bus. Such theories not only ignore the difference between what it is possible to do and what is so overwhelmingly difficult as to be almost impossible, but, far more important, they ignore the deep-rooted inclinations and preferences of free and vital people. Plans based on inflexible theories will never succeed in England while the national character remains as it is. So it is certain that, while some of the more isolated hamlets may have to disappear, the improvement of the social life of the countryside lies essentially in the preservation and improvement of its villages.

The beauty of the traditional English village at its best is one of our most notable contributions to the achievements of civilization. If our new village building is to be worthy of the old, and is to be in harmony with it, we shall need to build very differently from what we

* The commonest size for a village in England, i.e. a population of 300-400, is about the minimum size to maintain in being a small school, a village hall, and other social institutions.

have done in the recent past. This does not mean that we should attempt to imitate the details of the old buildings, any more than new town building means that. Harmony in building does not lie in imitation. It lies in the maintenance of 'scale' and the use of suitable sympathetic materials. Providing that this harmony is achieved, our village buildings can be, and should be, buildings that are essentially of their own time. But the maintenance of true village character depends far more on the plan-forms of buildings in association than on the detailed design of the buildings themselves. The essential character of the English village lies in a simplicity of form that is immediately apprehensible. The complicated paraphernalia of 'formal' design in axes and cross-axes and the rest is as foreign to it as are the studied intricacies of 'informality'. In our village extensions in the future we shall need to build freely and straightforwardly, using simple forms like the terrace facing directly on to unfenced open greens. And as the building forms themselves should be simple and robust, so should the natural forms. In the village even more than elsewhere (but nevertheless everywhere) we will need to turn aside from the deplorable suburban vulgarity that has characterised all our planting during the last half century.

This consideration of natural forms brings us at last face to face with the real countryside, not the countryside as a sort of appendage to the town, but in its essential character as the scene of that agricultural-economic activity which is still, despite all change, the most vital and indispensable of our industries.

Industries? There surely is the key. For the days are past when farming could be regarded as the last occupational stronghold of ancient custom and staunch conservative individualism. The farm of the future will indeed be a factory, highly organised for maximum production within the carefully considered limits of the

H

fertility of its land, and equipped with all the mechanical means that are necessary to its efficient working.

What will be the effect of this development on the landscape? It is hard to say. Few even of our agricultural experts would care to attempt to forecast with absolute certainty the precise directions of the future agricultural economy. Will large-scale farming with a new concentration on wheat-raising be the agricultural method of the future? Or will it be a concentration on stock-rearing and dairy produce through similar large-scale methods? Or again will the opposite of both these methods, intensive cultivation by small holding, prevail? Or will the present system of mixed farming on medium-sized units be brought up to a satisfactory standard of efficiency through the further development of co-operative marketing and the sharing of modern machinery? All these methods of improving the agricultural system have their advocates.

It is probable indeed that the future may see them all in operation. The extraordinary variety of soils, and the variations of climatic conditions in different parts of England, will more and more lead towards the organisation of agriculture on a regional basis. Some more or less accidental regionalization exists already. But "the essence of rational regionalization is that every characteristic district should be farmed as highly as possible on a system best suited to the peculiarities of soil and climate in relation to market facilities":* and we may therefore hope that in the future the whole agricultural economy will be organised on a plan determined through a national survey of soils and markets and a consideration of all other influencing factors.

When this has been done, and all the existing cultivated land throughout the country has been brought to its most efficient standard of productivity, then we may expect something of the eighteenth-century impulse

* Stapledon: *The Land.*

towards 'improvement' to recur in another direction, in the bringing of 'marginal' lands into greater usefulness. Large expanses of country await the hand of the twentieth-century improver. Sir George Stapledon has shown in his reclamation schemes in the Welsh hills how great areas of bracken-infested land can be converted to valuable pasturage, and he has proved that everywhere an enormous improvement may be effected in the quality of grasslands. We may well hope, then, that somewhere in the near future the industry of the countryside will advance, under the stimulus of this new tradition of improvement, to the position of honour and pride which is surely its right.

And what change will this economic re-establishment bring to the pictorial character of the rural scene? Again it is difficult to say. It may be probable that, under the more considered planning of the agricultural economy that has just been mentioned, the character of some districts may be changed. Some of the hedges and trees in these places may have to disappear in the reorganisation of fields into areas suitable for mechanical husbandry. If it is so, then we shall have to be content with the loss of them, for the countryside as a scene of economic activity is more important than the countryside as a pictorial composition—though this should by no means be permitted as a defence for unimaginative destruction. In the same way we shall have to accept in some places the transformation that will be wrought by large-scale afforestation—though, here too, the need for commercial timber must be weighed in the balance against other needs, and not allowed to destroy values greater than its own. That, indeed, must be the prime consideration everywhere in the countryside: and, in considering the claims of various activities which may produce long-lasting results, those claims will have to be weighed in the light of the public good measured in terms of future as well as immediate needs. As long as something like our present civilization remains, these needs will be social and aesthetic as well as economic. So the large-scale activities in the countryside, as well as in the towns, must be made subject to plans that have been drawn up in the national interest. Change there is bound to be. In our physical environment, as in our lives, a merely conservative preservation of a condition which has been reached at one particular point of time is bound to fail. The only policy of preservation that has any chance of success is through planned and clear-sighted growth. And if this cannot ensure the maintenance in their present shape of all today's familiar things, there is much to be thankful for as well as much to regret.

But the shape of things to come need by no means be unpleasant—their shaping is indeed in our own hands. And in any case no wide-scale transformation of the whole countryside is likely. It is far more probable that in most districts new opportunities of landscape adornment will arise out of the changed agricultural conditions. Let us hope that we shall be worthy of these opportunities and that through us the English countryside of hedgerows and trees, though it may be modified, will yet retain its essential simplicity and beauty, may be renewed in a new passion for genuine improvement, and may become the living memorial and testimony to our own character, as that which we have inherited was a testimony to the quality of the men who created it nearly two hundred years ago.

6. Alcester: Warwickshire

MEDIAEVAL

It is difficult today to form any clear picture of what the mediaeval town looked like as a whole. For the most part it must have been a jumble of strongly individualised buildings of wildly differing heights and sizes. The Shambles at York (9) shows what the more important commercial streets in the more important towns looked like. How rich, lively and full of incident and drama the best were can still be seen in Canterbury (7), Durham (8) and other cathedral cities, and in the Oxford sky line of today (12) in spite of all the subsequent additions that have been made to it. But the mediaeval builders could impose notable order on work which they conceived as a whole—witness the great cathedrals and churches, university buildings like the great court of Trinity College, Cambridge (11), and even the ground plans of their new towns.

As to the appearance of the countryside, it is even more difficult to picture that in the England of today. But the still-surviving open fields of Laxton (13) show clearly what it was like in the cultivated parts.

8. (*Above*) *Durham*

7. (*Opposite*) *Canterbury*

9. (*Above*) York

10. (*Above*) *Chichester*

11. (*Below*) *Trinity College, Cambridge*

12. (*Above*) *Oxford*

13. (*Below*) *Open Fields: Laxton, Nottinghamshire*

14. (*Above*) *Oxford*

15. Newcastle-on-Tyne

RENAISSANCE

The main contribution of the Renaissance to the art of building towns was the acknowledgement of the Street as the unit of design. The formal organisation of individual façades led naturally to the formal organisation of those in association. Alike in London (16) and in the provincial towns (17:18), the square, the crescent and the terrace became the characteristic method of building. Even in the slowly-growing towns (19:21) buildings generations apart in time were given an harmonious relationship of spirit. The general effect was one of robust urbanity. It truly expressed the English genius for order without regimentation, form without formality.

That was equally expressed in the villages of the countryside (22:23); and in the country estates where the 'grand manner' of the Continent (24) was abandoned for that peculiarly English creation, the country park (25). It was especially expressed in the humanisation of the ordinary countryside (1).

18. (*Above*) *Cheltenham*

16. (*Opposite top*) *Gray's Inn, London*

17. (*Opposite bottom*) *Taunton*

19. (*Above*) *King's Lynn*

20. (*Below*) *Blandford*

21. *(Above)* Deal

22. (*Above*) *Biddestone, Wilts.*

23. (*Below*) *Askham, Cumberland*

24. (*Above*) *Windsor Great Park*

25. (*Below*) *Stourhead, Wilts.*

HELL AND MIDDLESBROUGH

After the renaissance, darkness again and a nightmare. In Victorian England (for the most part) "the idea of the town as a focus of civilization, as the witness of the beauty and order and freedom that men can bring into their lives, had vanished from all minds."

26. (Opposite) Industrial Scene, Crook, Co. Durham
27. (Below) Middlesbrough   28. (Bottom) Byelaw Street, anywhere

The degradation of the traditional town inevitably led to the desire to escape from it. The new romanticism suggested that the countryside was the refuge. But in spite of the assistance afforded by the railway, the refuge could only be a cross between the two. So, as the degradation of the town proceeded, romantic suburbs and suburb-towns like Bournemouth (29) were built for the wealthy. Later a few industrialist-reformers began to build, for their workpeople, model villages in imitation of Bournemouth (30). Later again other reformers began building garden cities (31): and all the town-councils and all the speculating builders imitated them (32). Last century killed the civic ideal; this century established the suburban.

29. (Opposite) Bournemouth

30. (Below) Welwyn Garden City

31. *(Above) Garden Suburb: Bournvil*

32. (*Above*) *Road and Ribbon Suburbia*
33. (*Below*) *Land Settlement Suburbia*

141

The four great periods in the development of the English scene have been—first, the mediæval period of small informal town and bare and patchy landscape ; second, the renaissance period of the more composed and formalised town and the enriched informal countryside ; third, the age of the industrial revolution when the town was debased and brutalised ; and, most recently, the age of spreading suburbia, of Town-Country. How will the future scene develop?

Town-Country has proved to be an aesthetic void, a social wilderness. The need for the future, in a land as crowded as England, is to re-establish something of the traditional physical antithesis between town and country, so that each may be pure of its own kind. The best of the buildings of the last two decades have recovered something of the urbanity of the great age of town building. And town and country planning is now recognised as the essential basis for orderly progress towards an orderly environment for living.

34. (Below) Highpoint, Highgate, London

35. (*Above*) *Stratford-on-Avon*

36. (*Above*) *Streatham, London*
37. (*Opposite*) *Old and new: Camden Town, London*

38. (*Above*) *Sloane Square, London*

39. (*Above*) *Village College, Impington, Cambridge*

40. (*Below*) *Factory, Welwyn*

41. Oxford replanned

The architects of the buildings and projects shown in illustrations 5-41 are as follows:—5, Frederick Gibberd; 34, Messrs. Tecton; 35, F. R. S. & F. W. B. Yorke; 36, Frederick Gibberd; 37, Serge Chermayeff; 38, William Crabtree and others; 39, Walter Gropius and Maxwell Fry; 40, O. R. Salvisberg; 41, Thomas Sharp.

INDEX

149

Durham, 34, 35

Inclosure Acts, 53, 62

151

Printed in Great Britain by C. Tinling & Co. Ltd., Liverpool, London and Prescot.